# THE
# SMART
# TEENAGER

THIS PUZZLE BOOK BELONGS TO _____

# CONTENT

STANDING TALL ----------------------------------------------------5

CROSSWORD ----------------------------------------------- 8

KAKURO --------------------------------------------------15

CRYPTOGRAM ------------------------------------------23

FIND YOUR WAY OUT ------------------------------ 29

WORD SEARCH ----------------------------------------- 35

SUDOKU -----------------------------------------------------42

ANAGRAM ------------------------------------------------53

SQUARE SUM ---------------------------------------- 58

WORD TRAIN ----------------------------------------- 62

LITTLE WORDS -------------------------------------- 67

CITY LIMITS ------------------------------------------- 71

TRIVIA LADDER --------------------------------------- 74

ANSWER KEY ------------------------------------------ 77

    STANDING TALL ------------------------------------------78

    CROSSWORD --------------------------------------------- 79

    KAKURO --------------------------------------------------- 81

    CRYPTOGRAM --------------------------------------------- 83

    FIND YOUR WAY OUT -------------------------------------- 84

    WORD SEARCH ---------------------------------------------- 86

    SUDOKU ----------------------------------------------------87

    ANAGRAM ----------------------------------------------- 95

    SQUARE SUM ------------------------------------------ 96

    WORD TRAIN ------------------------------------------- 98

    LITTLE WORDS --------------------------------------- 99

    CITY LIMITS -------------------------------------------- 100

    TRIVIA LADDER -------------------------------------- 100

# Your Free Gift

As a way of thanking for your purchase, I am offering the e-copy of "Mind Maze" for free to my readers.

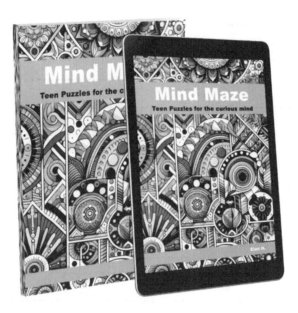

"Mind Maze" is a collection of Sudoku, Maze, Kakuro and Word Search puzzles with Solutions.

Solve puzzles to boost critical thinking, improve problem-solving skills, and resilience, prepare yourself for challenges in academics and beyond while experiencing a fun and rewarding mental workout.

To get instant access just go to:
https://bit.ly/TST-FreeGift

or scan the QR code below:

SCAN ME

# STANDING TALL!!

# STANDING TALL #1

GO AROUND STRIKING OFF NUMBERS THAT SATISFY THE CONDITIONS BELOW.
SOLUTION IS THAT ONE NUMBER UNSTRUCK, STANDING TALL AT THE END!

1. THE NUMBER IS DIVISIBLE BY 3
2. THE NUMBER IS DIVISIBLE BY 7
3. THE NUMBER ENDS WITH A 0
4. THE NUMBER ENDS WITH A 5
5. THE NUMBER IS DIVISIBLE BY 11
6. ALL POSSIBLE NUMBER OF DAYS IN A MONTH
7. THE NUMBER IS DIVISIBLE BY 8

| 147 | 12 | 500 | 999 | 2345 | 895 | 29 |
|------|------|------|------|------|------|------|
| 225 | 220 | 161 | 22 | 769 | 354 | 795 |
| 168 | 154 | 333 | 207 | 550 | 910 | 462 |
| 319 | 903 | 105 | 297 | 808 | 175 | 372 |
| 1010 | 429 | 707 | 123 | 133 | 88 | 824 |
| 180 | 55 | 473 | 308 | 805 | 303 | 1648 |
| 31 | 771 | 728 | 30 | 320 | 28 | 1111 |

# STANDING TALL #2

GO AROUND STRIKING OFF NUMBERS THAT ARE ANSWERS TO THE QUESTIONS BELOW.
SOLUTION IS THAT ONE NUMBER UNSTRUCK, STANDING TALL AT THE END!

| 9 | 15 | 18 | 12 | 5 | 366 | 30 |
|---|----|----|----|---|-----|----|
| 32 | 47 | 46 | 41 | 1000 | 24 | 7 |
| 29 | 6 | 50 | 16 | 19 | 128 | 60 |
| 10 | 53 | 1776 | 11 | 14 | 28 | 10 |
| 50 | 911 | 365 | 988 | 13 | 40 | 20 |
| 3 | 35 | 43 | 404 | 99 | 69 | 70 |
| 22 | 2 | 25 | 31 | 1994 | 511 | 8 |

1. NUMBER OF LETTERS IN WEEKDAYS
2. NUMBER OF LETTERS IN MONTHS
3. A DOZEN
4. POSSIBLE NUMBER OF DAYS IN A MONTH
5. POSSIBLE NUMBER OF DAYS IN A YEAR
6. JUNETEENTH IS CELEBRATED ON THIS DAY OF JUNE
7. THE INKTOBER MONTH IN NUMERALS
8. AN UNLUCKY NUMBER
9. 2 MINIMUM AGES FOR DRIVING LICENSE
10. IF GEORGE WASHINGTON IS 1, WHAT IS JOE BIDEN?
11. THIS APOLLO LANDED THE FIRST MEN IN SPACE
12. NUMBER OF US STATES
13. IF AN INTERNET USER FOLLOWS A BROKEN OR DEAD LINK, THEY WILL TYPICALLY FIND AN ERROR PAGE WITH WHICH NUMBER ERROR MESSAGE
14. US EMERGENCY CONTACT NUMBER
15. WHICH AGE DO YOU HAVE TO REACH TO BE ELIGIBLE TO BECOME PRESIDENT OF THE UNITED STATES
16. SEXAGENARIAN IS ABOVE THIS AGE
17. SEPTUAGENARIAN IS ABOVE THIS AGE
18. HOW MANY NUMBERS FROM 1 TO 99 DO NOT HAVE A,B,C,D?
19. HOW MANY MILLIONS MAKE A BILLION?
20. IF APPLE IS 5 AND BANANA IS 6, WHAT IS UNCOPYRIGHTABLE?
21. 4!
22. SUICIDE PREVENTION NUMBER

23. AT WHAT FAHRENHEIT DOES WATER FREEZE?
24. THE YEAR OF US INDEPENDENCE
25. NUMBER OF YEARS THAT MAKE A SILVER JUBILEE
26. NUMBER OF YEARS THAT MAKE A GOLDEN JUBILEE
27. TWITTER'S NEW NAME IS ROMAN NUMERIC FORM OF THIS NUMBER
28. HIGHEST PRIME NUMBER LESSER THAN 55
29. PRIME NUMBERS BETWEEN 40 AND 50
30. 2 CUBED + 2 SQUARED + 2!
31. ONE QUARTER OF ONE THIRD OF 24
32. HOW MANY OZ MAKES A GALLON?
33. SUM OF FIRST 6 NUMBERS OF A FIBONACCI SERIES STARTING WITH 1,1
34. YEAR WHEN PULP FICTION, THE SHAWSHANK REDEMPTION, AND JURASSIC PARK RELEASED
35. SUMMER OF '_ _?
36. ONE ANGLE IN A RIGHT TRIANGLE IS 49, WHAT IS THE OTHER ANGLE?

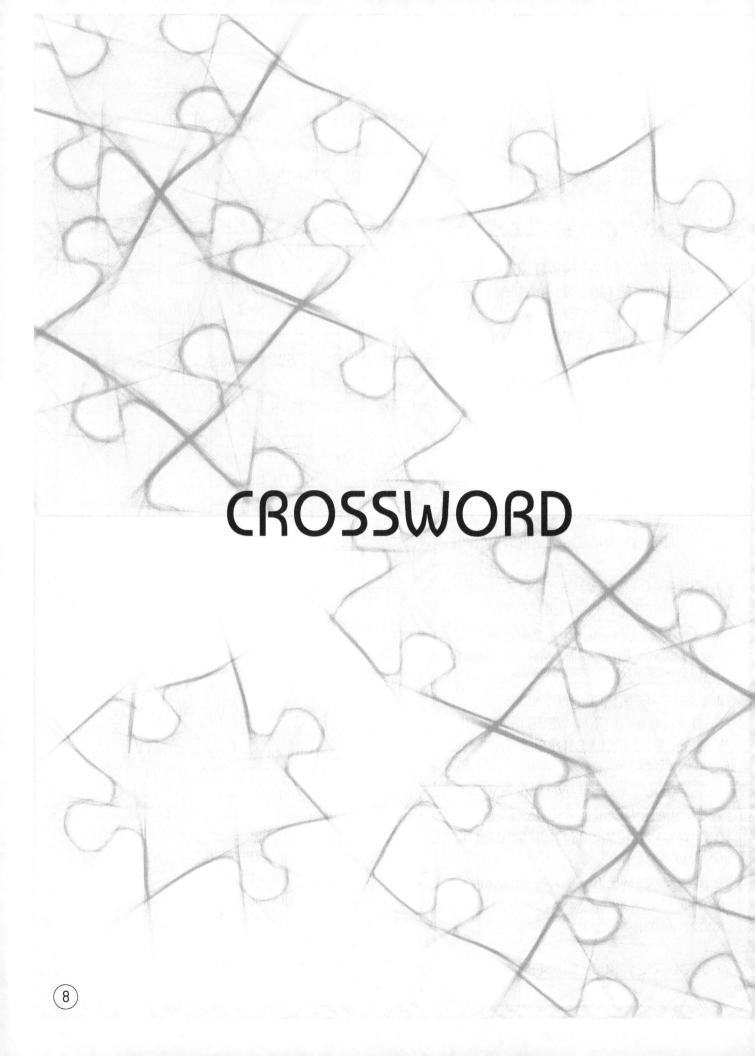

# CROSSWORD

## ACROSS ▶

1. THE PLANET WE LIVE ON
3. THE STUDY OF LIVING ORGANISMS
4. THE SMALLEST UNIT OF AN ELEMENT THAT RETAINS ITS CHEMICAL PROPERTIES
7. THE NATURAL SATELLITE OF THE EARTH
9. A GROUP OF SIMILAR CELLS WORKING TOGETHER TO PERFORM A SPECIFIC FUNCTION
2. THE BASIC UNIT OF HEREDITY IN LIVING ORGANISMS
11. THE PROCESS BY WHICH AN ORGANISM DEVELOPS FROM A SINGLE-CELLED ZYGOTE TO A MULTICELLULAR ORGANISM
12. THE STUDY OF ROCKS AND THE EARTH'S CRUST
13. THE STUDY OF THE UNIVERSE AND CELESTIAL OBJECTS
16. THE PROCESS OF CONVERTING FOOD INTO ENERGY

## DOWN ▼

2. THE FORCE THAT ATTRACTS TWO OBJECTS TOWARD EACH OTHER
1. A SUBSTANCE THAT CANNOT BE BROKEN DOWN INTO SIMPLER SUBSTANCES
5. THE PROCESS BY WHICH PLANTS MAKE THEIR OWN FOOD USING SUNLIGHT
6. THE STUDY OF MATTER AND ITS MOTION THROUGH SPACE AND TIME
8. A SUBSTANCE THAT SPEEDS UP A CHEMICAL REACTION
10. THE STUDY OF THE EARTH'S ATMOSPHERE AND WEATHER
14. A SUBSTANCE THAT SPEEDS UP A REACTION WITHOUT BEING CONSUMED IN THE PROCESS
15. A SUBSTANCE THAT CONDUCTS ELECTRICITY AND IS ALTERED OR DESTROYED IN THE PROCESS
17. A DEVICE USED TO MAGNIFY SMALL OBJECTS
18. THE STUDY OF THE COMPOSITION AND PROPERTIES OF MATTER

## ACROSS ▶

2. A SHAPE WITH THREE SIDES
3. A NUMBER THAT CAN BE DIVIDED EVENLY BY 2
5. A FOUR-SIDED FIGURE
6. THE RESULT OF MULTIPLYING TWO OR MORE NUMBERS
8. THE HIGHEST COMMON FACTOR OF TWO OR MORE NUMBERS
9. A POLYGON WITH SIX SIDES
4. THE TOTAL SPACE ENCLOSED BY THE BOUNDARIES OF A TWO-DIMENSIONAL SHAPE
13. A WHOLE NUMBER GREATER THAN 1 THAT CANNOT BE EXACTLY DIVIDED BY ANY WHOLE NUMBER OTHER THAN ITSELF AND 1
15. THE STUDY OF SHAPES, SIZES, AND PROPERTIES OF FIGURES AND SPACES
17. A SEQUENCE OF NUMBERS WHERE EACH TERM IS THE SUM OF THE TWO PRECEDING ONES

## DOWN ▼

1. THE BASIC UNIT OF COUNTING
4. THE OPPOSITE OF SUBTRACTION
7. A NUMBER THAT CANNOT BE EXPRESSED AS A FRACTION
2. A STRAIGHT LINE THAT TOUCHES A CURVE AT A SINGLE POINT WITHOUT CROSSING IT
10. A NUMBER THAT IS THE SAME FORWARD AND BACKWARD
11. A MATHEMATICAL STATEMENT THAT SHOWS THE EQUALITY OF TWO EXPRESSIONS
12. A QUANTITY REPRESENTING THE POWER TO WHICH A GIVEN NUMBER OR EXPRESSION IS TO BE RAISED
14. A NUMBER THAT IS NOT A FRACTION; A WHOLE NUMBER
6. A FRACTION IN WHICH THE NUMERATOR IS SMALLER THAN THE DENOMINATOR
16. THE DISTANCE AROUND A CIRCLE

# CROSSWORD #3
## GEOGRAPHY

ROAD TRIP

## ACROSS ▶

1. THE VEHICLE USED FOR A ROAD TRIP
3. THE PLANNED PATH OR DIRECTION FOR A ROAD TRIP
4. THE PERSON OPERATING THE VEHICLE DURING THE ROAD TRIP
6. FUEL NEEDED TO POWER THE CAR.
7. A MAJOR ROAD FOR HIGH-SPEED TRAVEL DURING A ROAD TRIP
8. A DESIGNATED AREA ALONG THE HIGHWAY FOR TRAVELERS TO TAKE A BREAK
10. A PICTURESQUE SIGHT ALONG THE ROAD TRIP ROUTE
11. INTERESTING PLACES TO VISIT ON THE WAY
13. TRAFFIC SIGNS PROVIDING INFORMATION AND DIRECTIONS
17. A TEMPORARY ROUTE USED TO AVOID A CLOSED ROAD OR OBSTRUCTION

## DOWN ▼

2. A GUIDE USED FOR NAVIGATION DURING A ROAD TRIP
5. A PERSON TRAVELING IN THE CAR BUT NOT DRIVING
9. THE NUMBER OF MILES TRAVELED DURING THE ROAD TRIP
12. THE ENDPOINT OR GOAL OF THE ROAD TRIP
14. THE ACT OF GOING ON A JOURNEY, LIKE A ROAD TRIP
15. BAGS AND BELONGINGS PACKED FOR THE TRIP
7. A PLACE TO STAY OVERNIGHT DURING THE ROAD TRIP
16. A DESIGNATED AREA FOR CAMPING ALONG THE ROAD TRIP ROUTE
18. THE PROCESS OF FINDING THE WAY DURING THE ROAD TRIP
19. A QUICK STOP FOR FUEL, FOOD, OR RESTROOM BREAK

## SOCCER

## ACROSS ▶

1. THE OBJECT OF THE GAME, SCORING IT WINS MATCHES
2. THE ROUND OBJECT KICKED IN SOCCER
3. A GROUP OF PLAYERS WORKING TOGETHER TO WIN A MATCH
5. SOMEONE ACTIVELY PARTICIPATING IN THE GAME
6. THE OFFICIAL WHO ENFORCES THE RULES DURING A MATCH
7. A PERSON WHO TRAINS AND GUIDES THE TEAM
8. THE LEADER OF THE TEAM, OFTEN IDENTIFIED BY AN ARMBAND
4. THE ACT OF KICKING THE BALL TO A TEAMMATE
14. A TECHNIQUE WHERE A PLAYER HITS THE BALL WITH THEIR HEAD
6. THE BREAK BETWEEN THE TWO HALVES OF A SOCCER MATCH

## DOWN ▼

4. THE PLAYING FIELD IN SOCCER
9. THE PLAYER WHO GUARDS THE GOAL AND TRIES TO PREVENT GOALS
10. THE SHIRT WORN BY PLAYERS DURING THE GAME
11. SHOES WITH STUDS WORN BY PLAYERS FOR BETTER GRIP ON THE PITCH
12. AN INFRINGEMENT OF THE RULES, OFTEN LEADING TO A FREE-KICK OR PENALTY
13. THE SKILLFUL MANEUVERING OF THE BALL BY A PLAYER
15. A DEFENSIVE MOVE TO TAKE THE BALL AWAY FROM AN OPPONENT
17. ADDITIONAL TIME ADDED TO COMPENSATE FOR STOPPAGES DURING EACH HALF
18. A PLAYER BROUGHT INTO THE GAME TO REPLACE ANOTHER
19. A POSITION IN WHICH AN ATTACKING PLAYER IS CLOSER TO THE OPPONENT'S GOAL THAN THE LAST DEFENDER

## ACROSS ▶

2. THE RATIO OF THE CIRCUMFERENCE OF A CIRCLE TO ITS DIAMETER

7. A POLYGON WITH EIGHT SIDES

4. A RING-SHAPED CORAL REEF, ISLAND, OR SERIES OF ISLETS

9. A FREE SHOT ON GOAL FROM THE PENALTY SPOT, AWARDED FOR A MAJOR FOUL

10. A SUBSTANCE THAT DISSOLVES IN A SOLVENT TO FORM A SOLUTION

5. A LINE SEGMENT THAT JOINS TWO POINTS ON A CIRCLE

11. THIS EXTENDS INFINITELY IN BOTH DIRECTIONS

13. A POINT OF LAND THAT EXTENDS INTO A RIVER, LAKE, OR OCEAN

14. TO TRAVEL AROUND A NEW PLACE AND DISCOVER IT DURING THE ROAD TRIP

15. VEHICLES MOVING ON THE ROAD, SOMETIMES CAUSING DELAYS

16. THE STRUCTURE BEHIND THE GOAL WHERE THE BALL IS KICKED TO SCORE

## DOWN ▼

1. THE BASIC UNIT OF LIFE

3. A GROUP OR CHAIN OF ISLANDS

4. READY TO TAKE RISKS AND EXPLORE NEW PLACES ON THE ROAD TRIP

5. A SET-PIECE TAKEN FROM THE CORNER OF THE FIELD IN SOCER

6. A SYSTEM OF CELLS, TISSUES, AND ORGANS THAT WORK TOGETHER TO PERFORM VARIOUS FUNCTIONS IN A LIVING ORGANISM

8. A BOOK OR RESOURCE PROVIDING INFORMATION ABOUT THE DESTINATIONS

12. A FLAT ELEVATED AREA OF LAND

17. THE TOOL USED BY THE REFEREE TO SIGNAL THE START, STOP, OR RESTART OF PLAY IN SOCCER

# KAKURO

# KAKURO

KAKURO IS A LOGIC BASED NUMBER PLACEMENT PUZZLE, AT TIMES REFERRED TO AS THE NUMBER CROSSWORD.

HOW TO PLAY:

1. PLACE NUMBERS IN THE EMPTY WHITE SQUARES OF THE GRID
2. USE THE NUMBERS 1-9 ONLY AND NUMBERS CANNOT REPEAT IN ANY CROSS OR DOWN RUN OF SQUARES
3. THE NUMBERS IN EACH RUN OF SQUARES MUST SUM TO THE NUMBER GIVEN AT THE START OF THAT RUN

## EXAMPLE:

1. CONSIDER VERTICAL SECTIONS C1, C2, C3
A+D SHOULD EQUAL 7, A AND D SHOULD BE UNIQUE
B+E SHOULD EQUAL 14, B AND E SHOULD BE UNIQUE
C+F+J+K+L+M SHOULD EQUAL 27, C, F, J, K, L AND M SHOULD BE UNIQUE

2. CONSIDER HORIZONTAL SECTIONS R1 AND R2
A+B+C SHOULD EQUAL 18, A, B, C SHOULD BE UNIQUE
D+E+F+G+H+I SHOULD EQUAL 30, D,E,F,G,H AND I SHOULD BE UNIQUE

3. CONSIDER SQUARE N, IT IS THE ONLY SQUARE UNDER SUM 5, IT CAN BE FILLED WITH 5 RIGHT AWAY

# KAKURO #1

# KAKURO #2

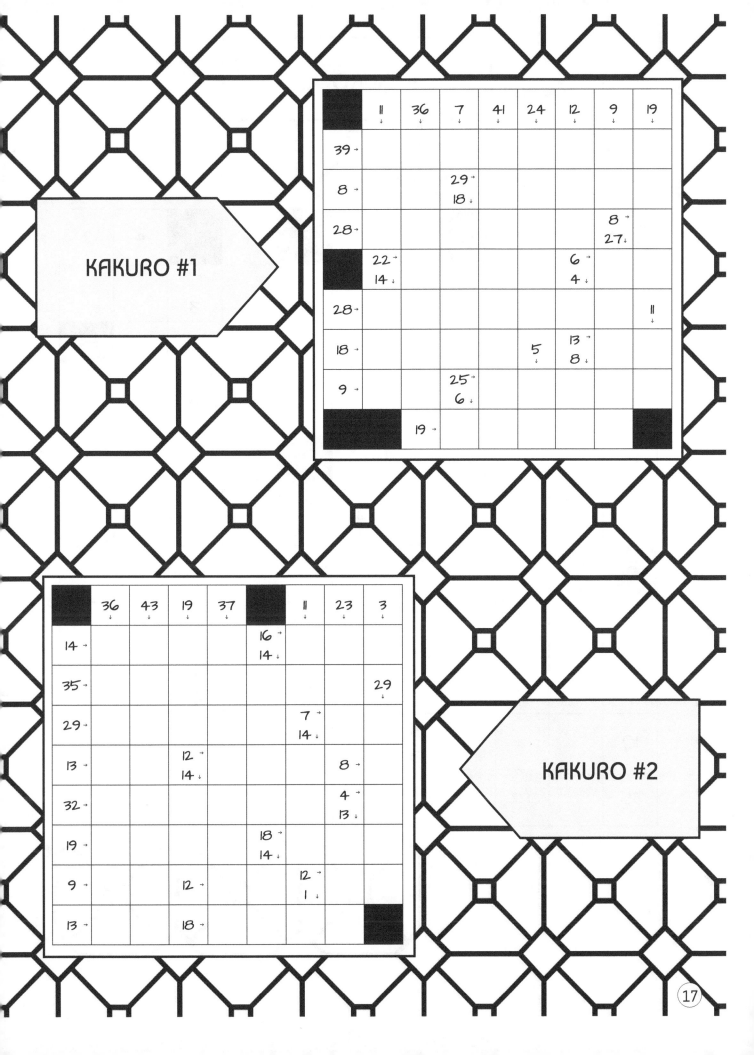

# KAKURO #3

| | 19↓ | 38↓ | ■ | 2↓ | 19↓ | ■ | 4↓ | ■ | 4↓ | 2↓ |
|---|---|---|---|---|---|---|---|---|---|---|
| 13→ | | | 5→ | | | 4→ 5↓ | | 5→ 3↓ | | |
| 5→ | | | 27↓ | 7→ 13↓ | | | 4→ 8↓ | | | ■ |
| 37→ | | | | | | | | 19↓ | 29↓ | 14↓ |
| 26→ | | | | | | ■ | 15→ 28↓ | | | |
| 13→ | | | | | 4↓ | 19→ 22↓ | | | | |
| ■ | 14→ 16↓ | | | 30→ 11↓ | | | | | | |
| 1→ | | 14→ 21↓ | | | 8→ 15↓ | | | 13→ | | |
| 40→ | | | | | | | | 1→ 6↓ | | 10↓ |
| 10→ | | | 1↓ | 14→ 3↓ | | | | | 1→ 5↓ | |
| 35→ | | | | | | | | 14→ | | |

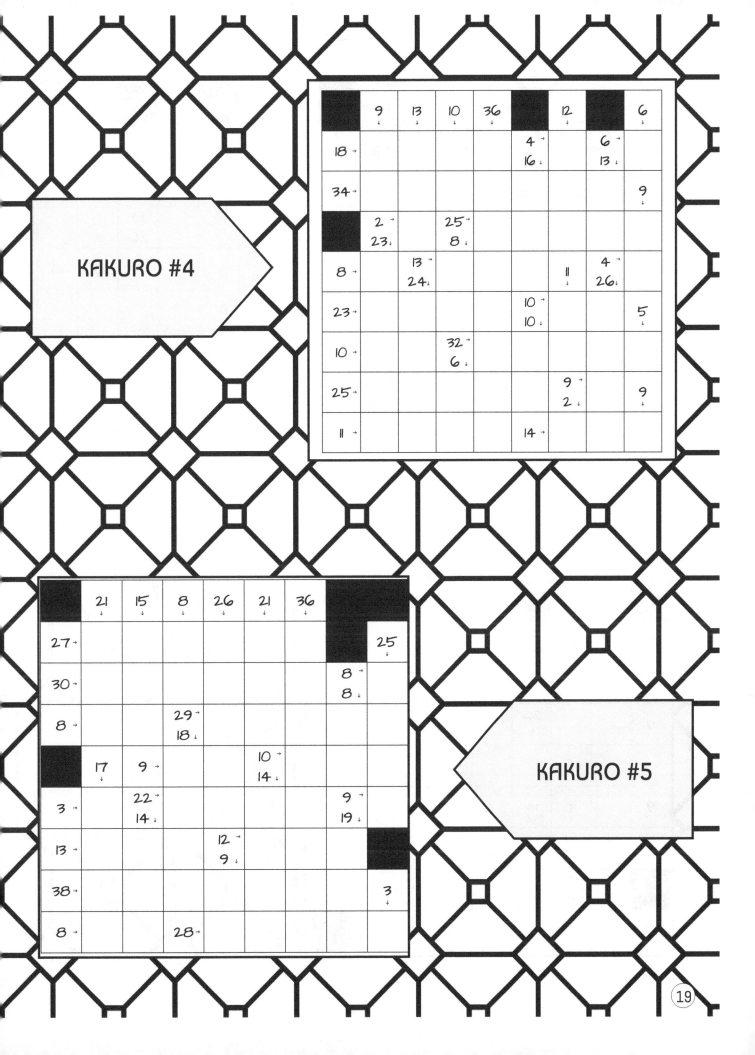

KAKURO #4

KAKURO #5

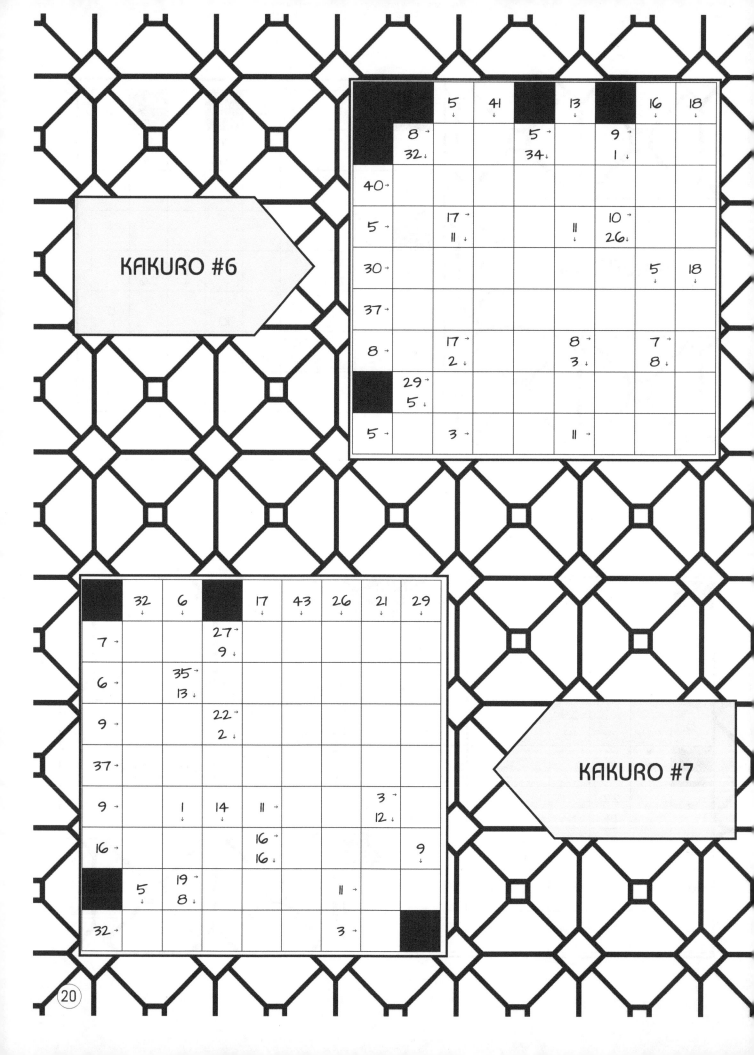

## KAKURO #6

| | | 5↓ | 41↓ | | 13↓ | | 16↓ | 18↓ |
|---|---|---|---|---|---|---|---|---|
| | 8→ 32↓ | | | 5→ 34↓ | | 9→ 1↓ | | |
| 40→ | | | | | | | | |
| 5→ | | 17→ 11↓ | | | 11↓ | 10→ 26↓ | | |
| 30→ | | | | | | | 5↓ | 18↓ |
| 37→ | | | | | | | | |
| 8→ | | 17→ 2↓ | | | 8→ 3↓ | | 7→ 8↓ | |
| | 29→ 5↓ | | | | | | | |
| 5→ | | 3→ | | | | 11→ | | |

## KAKURO #7

| | 32↓ | 6↓ | | 17↓ | 43↓ | 26↓ | 21↓ | 29↓ |
|---|---|---|---|---|---|---|---|---|
| 7→ | | | 27→ 9↓ | | | | | |
| 6→ | | 35→ 13↓ | | | | | | |
| 9→ | | | 22→ 2↓ | | | | | |
| 37→ | | | | | | | | |
| 9→ | | 1↓ | 14↓ | 11→ | | | 3→ 12↓ | |
| 16→ | | | | 16→ 16↓ | | | | 9↓ |
| | 5↓ | 19→ 8↓ | | | | | 11→ | |
| 32→ | | | | | 3→ | | | |

20

# KAKURO #8

| | 2↓ | 15↓ | 1↓ | 20↓ | 12↓ | 28↓ | 38↓ | 10↓ | ■ | 27↓ |
|---|---|---|---|---|---|---|---|---|---|---|
| 38→ | | | | | | | | | 2→ | |
| ■ | 6→ 1↓ | | 21→ | | | | | | 9→ 42↓ | |
| 1→ | | 16↓ | 21→ 7↓ | | | | | 12→ 10↓ | | |
| ■ | 6→ | | | | 22→ 31↓ | | | | | |
| ■ | 5→ 29↓ | | | 35→ 21↓ | | | | | | |
| 28→ | | | | | | 3→ 4↓ | | 10→ 10↓ | | |
| 14→ | | | 30→ 19↓ | | | | | | 12↓ | |
| 3→ | | 20→ 8↓ | | | | 11↓ | 11→ | | | |
| 18→ | | | | 8→ 6↓ | | | 12→ 7↓ | | | |
| 41→ | | | | | | | | 11→ | | |

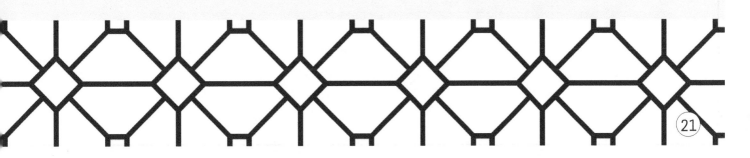

# KAKURO - FUN FACTS

1. KAKURO IS OFTEN CONSIDERED AS THE MATHEMATICAL TRANSLITERATION OF CROSSWORD
2. KAKURO IS KNOWN BY OTHER NAMES AS CROSS SUM AND CROSS ADDITION
3. KAKURO PUZZLES APPEAR IN NEARLY 100 JAPANESE MAGAZINES AND NEWSPAPERS
4. KAKURO REMAINED THE MOST POPULAR LOGIC PUZZLE IN JAPANESE PRINTED PRESS UNTIL 1992, WHEN SUDOKU TOOK THE TOP SPOT

# CRYPTOGRAM

# CRYPTOGRAM #1

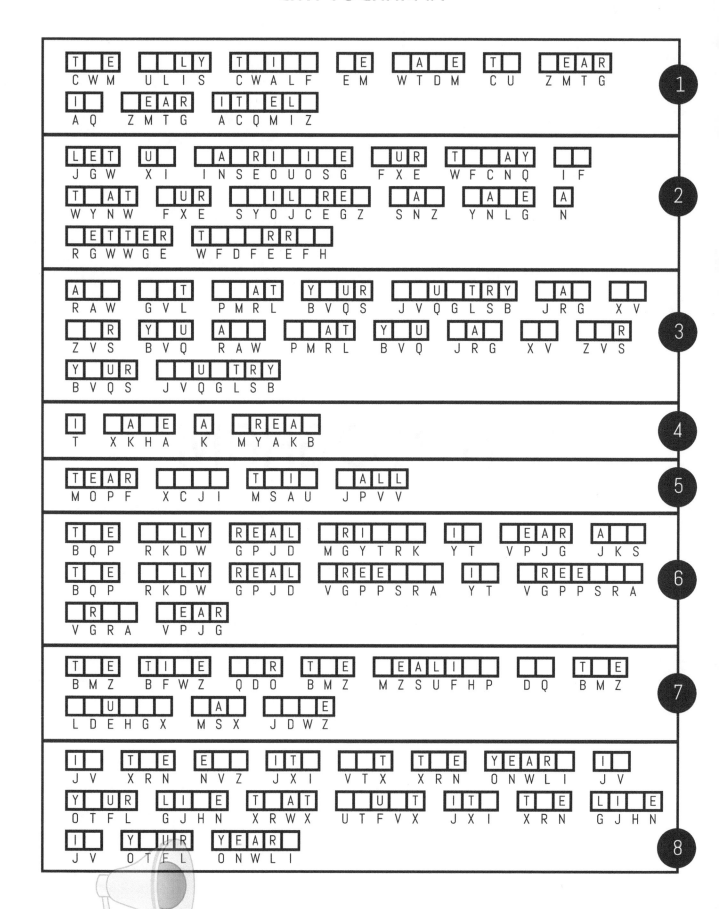

**1.**
T_E _ _LY T_I_ _ _E _A_E T_ _EAR
CWM  ULIS CWALF  EM  WTDM  CU  ZMTG
I_ _EAR IT_EL_
AQ  ZMTG  ACQMIZ

**2.**
LET _U_ _A_RI_IE_ _UR T_ _AY _ _
JGW  XI  INSEOUOSG  FXE  WFCNQ  IF
T_AT _UR _ _ILRE_ _A_ _AE A_
WYNW  FXE  SYOJCEGZ  SNZ  YNLG  N
_ETTER T_ _ _RR _ _
RGWWGE  WFDFEEFH

**3.**
A_ _ _ _T _ _AT Y_UR _ _U_TRY _A_ _ _
RAW  GVL  PMRL  BVQS  JVQGLSB  JRG  XV
_ _R Y_U A_ _ _ _AT Y_U _A_ _ _ _R
ZVS  BVQ  RAW  PMRL  BVQ  JRG  XV  ZVS
Y_UR _ _U_TRY
BVQS  JVQGLSB

**4.**
I _A_E A _REA_
T  XKHA  K  MYAKB

**5.**
TEAR _ _ _ _ T_I _ALL
MOPF  XCJI  MSAU  JPVV

**6.**
T_E _ _LY REAL _RI_ _ _ I_ _EAR A_ _
BQP  RKDW  GPJD  MGYTRK  YT  VPJG  JKS
T_E _ _LY REAL _REE_ _ I_ _REE_ _ _
BQP  RKDW  GPJD  VGPPSRA  YT  VGPPSRA
_R_ _ _EAR
VGRA  VPJG

**7.**
T_E TI_E_ _R TE_ _EALI_ _ _ _ T_E
BMZ  BFWZ  QDO  BMZ  MZSUFHP  DQ  BMZ
_ _U_ _ _A_ _ _ _E
LDEHGX  MSX  JDWZ

**8.**
I_ T_E E_ _ IT _ _T T_E YEAR_ I_
JV  XRN  NVZ  JXI  VTX  XRN  ONWLI  JV
Y_UR LI_E T_AT _ _UT I_T T_E LI_E
OTFL  GJHN  XRWX  UTFVX  JXI  XRN  GJHN
I_ Y_UR YEAR_
JV  OTFL  ONWLI

QUOTES FROM WORLD LEADERS

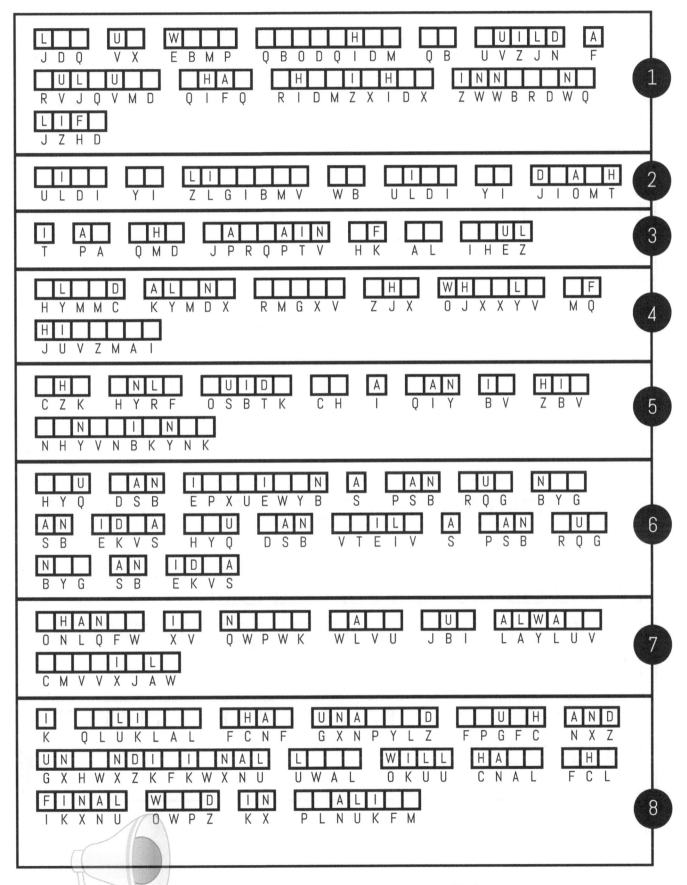

**1.**
L _ _ (JDQ)  _ U (VX)  W _ _ _ (EBMP)  _ _ _ _ _ H _ _ (QBODQIDM)  _ _ (QB)  _ U I L D (UVZJN)  A (F)
_ U L _ _ _ _ (RVJQVMD)  _ H A _ (QIFQ)  _ _ _ _ _ _ _ _ _ (RIDMZXIDX)  _ I N N _ _ _ _ N (ZWWBRDWQ)
L I F _ (JZHD)

**2.**
_ _ I _ (ULDI)  _ I (YI)  L I _ _ _ _ _ (ZLGIBMV)  _ _ (WB)  _ _ I _ (ULDI)  _ I (YI)  _ D _ A _ H (JIOMT)

**3.**
I (T)  _ A _ (PA)  _ H _ (QMD)  _ A _ _ A I N (JPRQPTV)  _ F (HK)  _ _ (AL)  _ _ _ U L (IHEZ)

**4.**
_ L _ _ D (HYMMC)  A L _ N _ (KYMDX)  _ _ _ _ _ (RMGXV)  _ H _ (ZJX)  W H _ _ L _ (OJXXYV)  _ F (MQ)
H I _ _ _ _ _ (JUVZMAI)

**5.**
_ H _ (CZK)  _ N L _ (HYRF)  _ U I D _ (OSBTK)  _ _ (CH)  _ A (I)  _ A N (QIY)  _ I (BV)  _ H I _ (ZBV)
_ _ _ _ _ N _ _ N _ (NHYVNBKYNK)

**6.**
_ _ U (HYQ)  _ A N (DSB)  I _ _ _ _ _ _ N (EPXUEWYB)  _ A (S)  _ A N (PSB)  _ U _ (RQG)  _ N _ (BYG)
A N (SB)  _ I D _ A (EKVS)  _ _ U (HYQ)  _ A N (DSB)  _ _ I L _ (VTEIV)  _ A (S)  _ A N (PSB)  _ U _ (RQG)
N _ _ (BYG)  _ A N (SB)  _ I D _ A (EKVS)

**7.**
_ H A N (ONLQFW)  _ I (XV)  N _ _ _ _ (QWPWK)  _ A _ _ (WLVU)  _ U _ (JBI)  A L W A _ _ (LAYLUV)
_ _ _ _ _ I L (CMVVXJAW)

**8.**
I (K)  _ _ L I _ _ _ (QLUKLAL)  _ H A _ (FCNF)  U N A _ _ _ D (GXNPYLZ)  _ _ U H (FPGFC)  A N D (NXZ)
U N _ _ N D I _ I _ N A L (GXHWXZKFKWXNU)  L _ _ _ (UWAL)  W I L L (OKUU)  H A _ _ (CNAL)  _ H _ (FCL)
F I N A L (IKXNU)  W _ D (OWPZ)  I N (KX)  _ _ A L I _ _ (PLNUKFM)

# CRYPTOGRAM #3

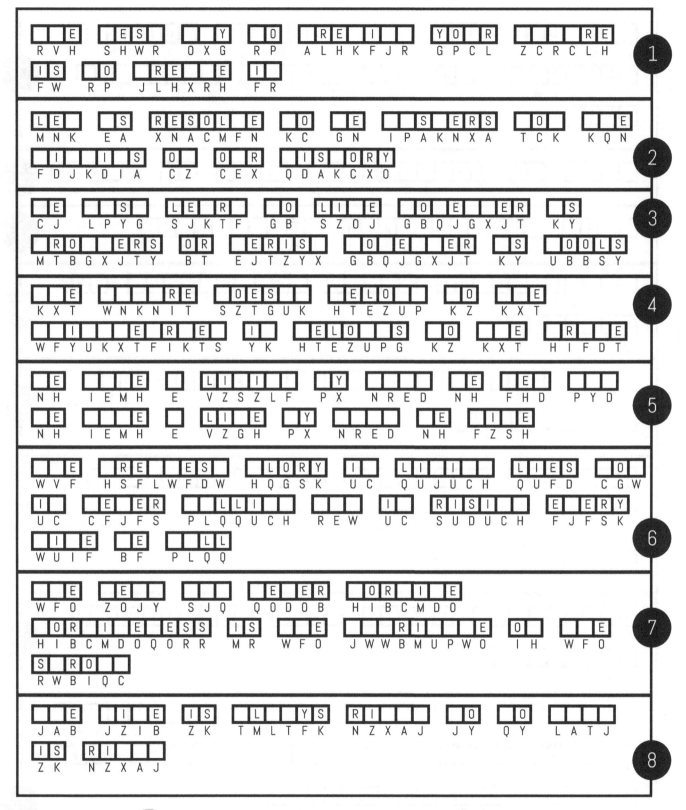

**1.**
```
 _E_   _ES_   __Y   _O   _RE__I_   YO_R   ____RE
 RVH   SHWR   OXG   RP   ALHKFJR   GPCL   ZCRCLH

 IS   _O   _RE__E_   I_
 FW   RP   JLHXRH    FR
```

**2.**
```
 LE_   _S   RESOL_E   _O   _E   __S_ERS   _O_   _ _E
 MNK   EA   XNACMFN   KC   GN   IPAKNXA   TCK   KQN

 _I_ _I_S   O_   O_R   _IS_OR_
 FDJKDIA    CZ   CEX   QDAKCXO
```

**3.**
```
 _E   __S_   LE_R_   _O   LI_E   _O_E_ER   _S
 CJ   LPYG   SJKTF   GB   SZOJ   GBQJGXJT   KY

 _RO__ERS   OR   _ERIS_   _O_E_ER   _S   _OOLS
 MTBGXJTY   BT   EJTZYX   GBQJGXJT   KY   UBBSY
```

**4.**
```
 _ _E   _ _ _ _RE   _OES_ _   _ELO_ _   _O   _ _E
 KXT    WNKNIT      SZTGUK    HTEZUP     KZ   KXT

 _ _I_ _ _ _ _RE_   I_   _ELO_ _S   _O   _ _E   _R_ _E
 WFYUKXTFIKTS       YK   HTEZUPG    KZ   KXT   HIFDT
```

**5.**
```
 _E   _ _E_   _   LI_I_ _   _Y   _ _ _ _   _E   _E_   _ _ _
 NH   IEMH   E   VZSZLF    PX   NRED     NH   FHD   PYD

 _E   _ _E_   _   LI_E   _Y   _ _ _ _   _E   _I_E
 NH   IEMH   E   VZGH   PX   NRED     NH   FZSH
```

**6.**
```
 _ _E   _RE_ _ES_   _LORY   I_   LI_I_ _   LIES   _O_
 WVF    HSFLWFDW    HQGSK    UC   QUJUCH    QUFD   CGW

 I_   _E_ER   _ _LLI_ _   _ _ _   I_   RISI_ _   E_ERY
 UC   CFJFS   PLQQUCH     REW   UC   SUDUCH    FJFSK

 _I_E   _E   _ _LL
 WUIF   BF   PLQQ
```

**7.**
```
 _ _E   _E_ _   _ _ _   _E_ER   _OR_I_E
 WFO    ZOJY   SJQ    QODOB   HIBCMDO

 _OR_I_E_ESS    IS   _ _E   _ _ _RI_ _ _E   O_   _ _E
 HIBCMDOQORR    MR   WFO   JWWBMUPWO        IH   WFO

 S_RO_ _
 RWBIQC
```

**8.**
```
 _ _E   _I_E   IS   _L_ _YS   RI_ _ _   _O   _O   _ _ _ _
 JAB    JZIB   ZK   TMLTFK    NZXAJ     JY   QY   LATJ

 IS   RI_ _ _
 ZK   NZXAJ
```

QUOTES FROM WORLD LEADERS

# CRYPTOGRAM #4

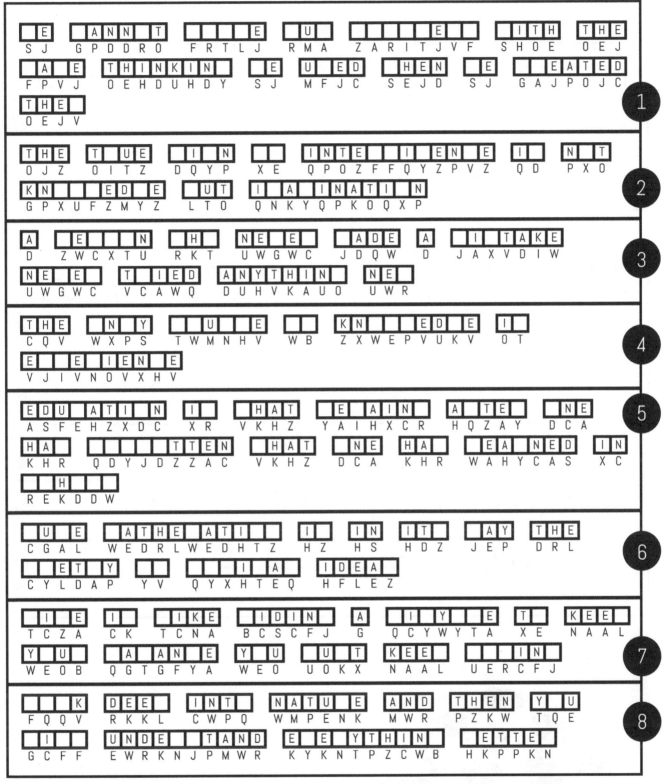

**1**

```
_E    _ANN_T   __L_E    _U   _____E__    _ITH   THE
SJ    GPDDRO   FRTLJ    RMA  ZARITJVF    SHOE   OEJ

_A_E    THINKIN_   _E   U_ED   _HEN   _E   _REATED
FPVJ    OEHDUHDY   SJ   MFJC   SEJD   SJ   GAJPOJC

THE_
OEJV
```

**2**

```
THE    T_UE    _I_N    __    INTE__I_EN_E    I_    N_T
OJZ    OITZ    DQYP    XE    QPOZFFQYZPVZ    QD    PXO

KN__ED_E      _UT    I_A_INATI_N
GPXUFZMYZ     LTO    QNKYQPKOQXP
```

**3**

```
A    _E__ON    _H_    NE_E_    _ADE    A    _I_TAKE
D    ZWCXTU    RKT   UWGWC    JDQW    D    JAXVDIW

NE_E_    T_IED    AN_THIN_    NE_
UWGWC    VCAWQ    DUHVKAUO    UWR
```

**4**

```
THE    _N_Y    __U__E    __    KN__ED_E    I_
CQV    WXPS    TWMNHV    WB    ZXWEPVUKV    OT

E__E_IEN_E
VJIVNOVXHV
```

**5**

```
EDU_ATI_N    I_    _HAT    _E_AIN_    A_TE_    _NE
ASFEHZXDC    XR    VKHZ    YAIHXCR    HQZAY    DCA

HA_    _____TTEN    _HAT    _NE    HA_    _EA_NED    IN
KHR    QDYJDZZAC    VKHZ    DCA    KHR    WAHYCAS    XC

__H___
REKDDW
```

**6**

```
_U_E    _ATHE_ATI__    I_    IN    IT_    _AY    THE
CGAL    WEDRLWEDHTZ    HZ    HS    HDZ    JEP    DRL

__ET_Y    __    ___I_A_    IDEA_
CYLDAP    YV    QYXHTEQ    HFLEZ
```

**7**

```
_I_E    I_    _IKE    _IDIN_    A    _I_Y__E    T_    KEE_
TCZA    CK    TCNA    BCSCFJ    G    QCYWYTA    XE    NAAL

Y_U_    _A_AN_E    Y_U    _U_T    KEE_    ___IN_
WEOB    QGTGFYA    WEO    UOKX    NAAL    UERCFJ
```

**8**

```
___K    DEE_    INT_    NATU_E    AND    THEN    Y_U
FQQV    RKKL    CWPQ    WMPENK    MWR    PZKW    TQE

_I__    UNDE__TAND    E_E_YTHIN_    _ETTE_
GCFF    EWRKNJPMWR    KYKNTPZCWB    HKPPKN
```

ALBERT EINSTEIN'S QUOTES

# CRYPTOGRAM #5

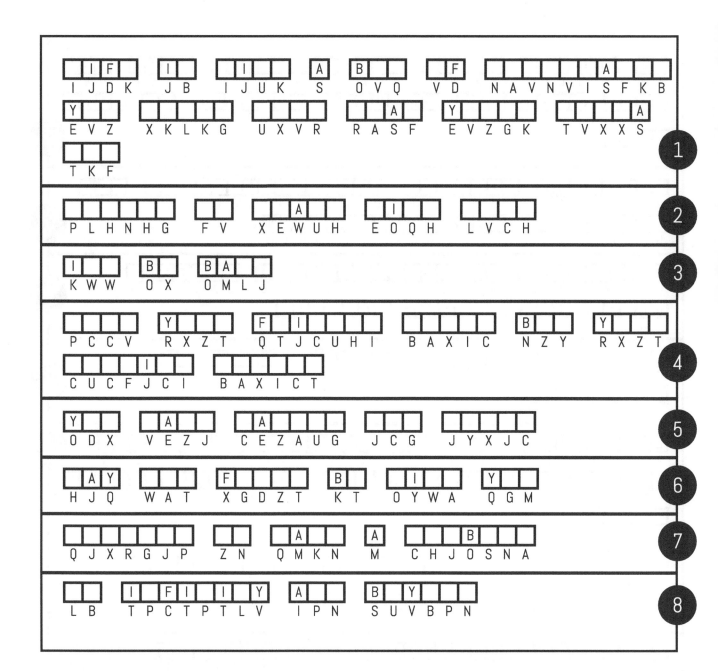

**1**

| `_IF_` | `I_` | `I__` | `A` | `B__` | `F_` | `_____A__` |
|---|---|---|---|---|---|---|
| I J D K | J B | I J U K | S | O V Q | V D | N A V N V I S F K B |

| `Y__` | `_____` | `____` | `___A_` | `Y____` | `____A` |
|---|---|---|---|---|---|
| E V Z | X K L K G | U X V R | R A S F | E V Z G K | T V X X S |

| `___` |
|---|
| T K F |

**2**

| `_____` | `__` | `__A__` | `_I__` | `____` |
|---|---|---|---|---|
| P L H N H G | F V | X E W U H | E O Q H | L V C H |

**3**

| `I__` | `_B_` | `BA__` |
|---|---|---|
| K W W | O X | O M L J |

**4**

| `____` | `Y___` | `F_I____` | `_____` | `B__` | `Y___` |
|---|---|---|---|---|---|
| P C C V | R X Z T | Q T J C U H I | B A X I C | N Z Y | R X Z T |

| `___I___` | `_____` |
|---|---|
| C U C F J C I | B A X I C T |

**5**

| `Y__` | `_A__` | `_A___` | `___` | `_____` |
|---|---|---|---|---|
| O D X | V E Z J | C E Z A U G | J C G | J Y X J C |

**6**

| `_AY` | `___` | `F___` | `B_` | `_I__` | `Y__` |
|---|---|---|---|---|---|
| H J Q | W A T | X G D Z T | K T | O Y W A | Q G M |

**7**

| `_____` | `__` | `_A__` | `A` | `___B___` |
|---|---|---|---|---|
| Q J X R G J P | Z N | Q M K N | M | C H J O S N A |

**8**

| `__` | `_I_I__Y` | `_A_` | `B_Y__` |
|---|---|---|---|
| L B | T P C T P T L V | I P N | S U V B P N |

HOLLYWOOD MOVIE PHRASES

28

# FIND YOUR WAY OUT!

# FIND YOUR WAY OUT #1

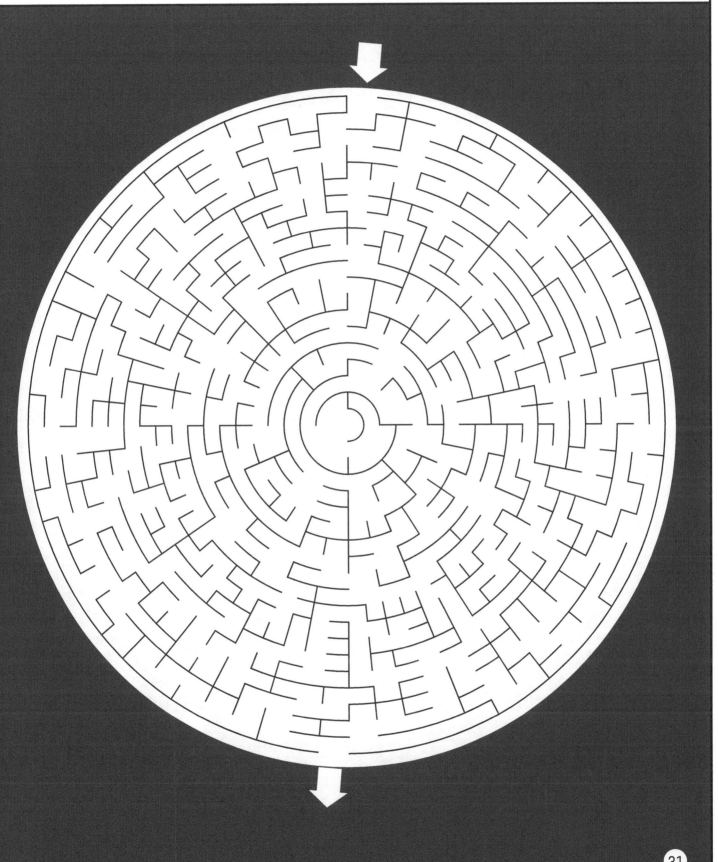

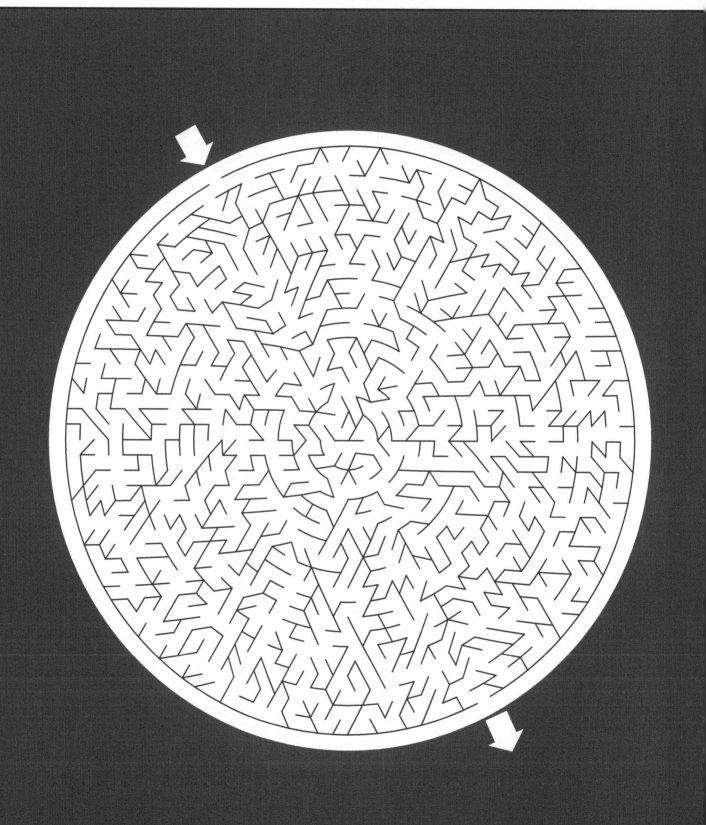

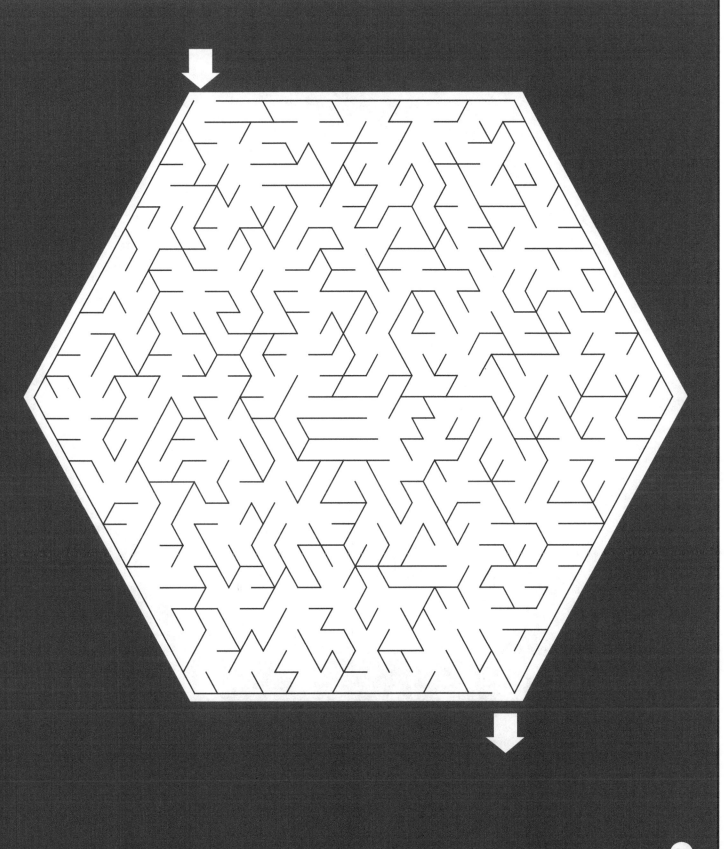

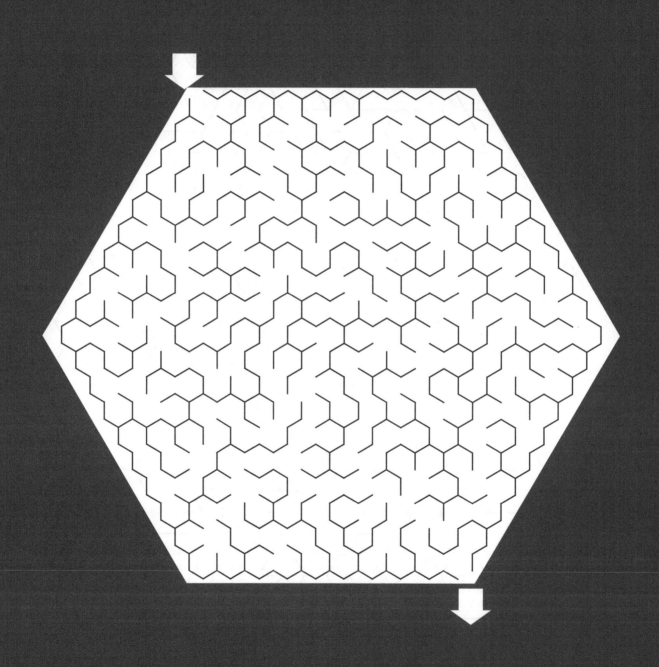

# WORD SEARCH

# WORD SEARCH #1

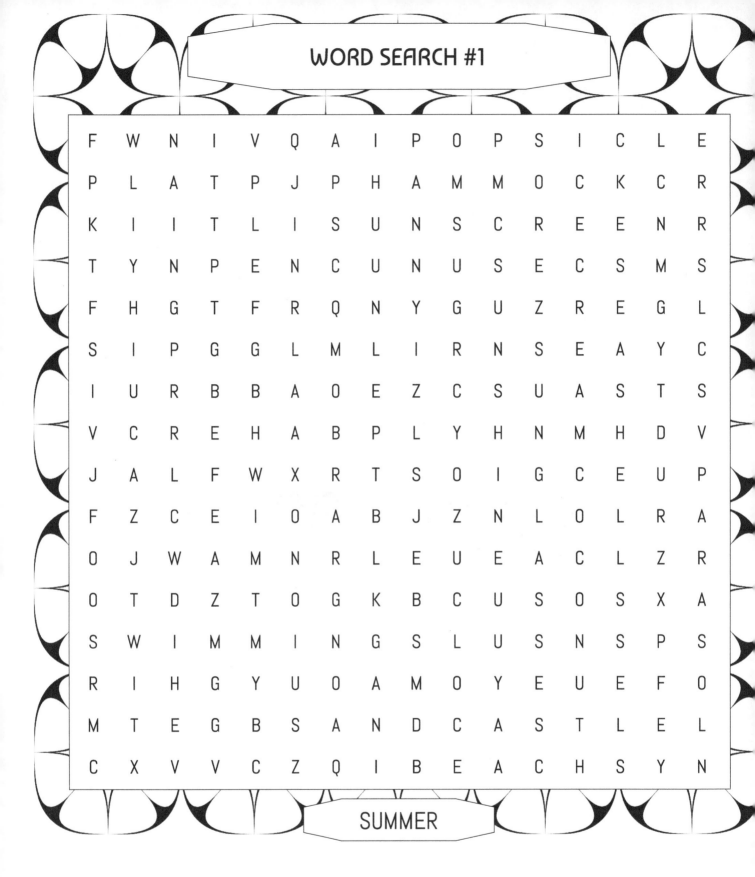

F W N I V Q A I P O P S I C L E
P L A T P J P H A M M O C K C R
K I I T L I S U N S C R E E N R
T Y N P E N C U N U S E C S M S
F H G T F R Q N Y G U Z R E G L
S I P G G L M L I R N S E A Y C
I U R B B A O E Z C S U A S T S
V C R E H A B P L Y H N M H D V
J A L F W X R T S O I G C E U P
F Z C E I O A B J Z N L O L R A
O J W A M N R L E U E A C L Z R
O T D Z T O G K B C U S O S X A
S W I M M I N G S L U S N S P S
R I H G Y U O A M O Y E U E F O
M T E G B S A N D C A S T L E L
C X V V C Z Q I B E A C H S Y N

SUMMER

SUNSHINE, BEACH, VACATION, SWIMMING, ICE CREAM, PICNIC, SANDCASTLE, FLIP
FLOPS, SUNGLASSES, BARBECUE, SUNSCREEN, SURFING, POPSICLE, SEA SHELLS,
WATERMELON, HAMMOCK, COCONUT, FIREWORKS, PARASOL, LEMONADE

# WORD SEARCH
## #2

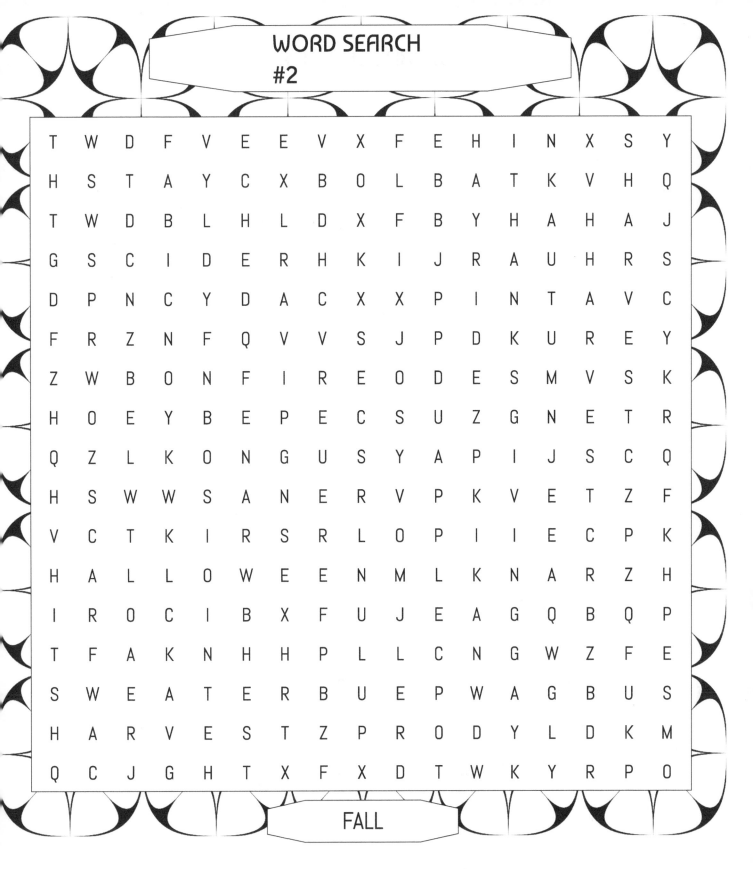

```
T  W  D  F  V  E  E  V  X  F  E  H  I  N  X  S  Y
H  S  T  A  Y  C  X  B  O  L  B  A  T  K  V  H  Q
T  W  D  B  L  H  L  D  X  F  B  Y  H  A  H  A  J
G  S  C  I  D  E  R  H  K  I  J  R  A  U  H  R  S
D  P  N  C  Y  D  A  C  X  X  P  I  N  T  A  V  C
F  R  Z  N  F  Q  V  V  S  J  P  D  K  U  R  E  Y
Z  W  B  O  N  F  I  R  E  O  D  E  S  M  V  S  K
H  O  E  Y  B  E  P  E  C  S  U  Z  G  N  E  T  R
Q  Z  L  K  O  N  G  U  S  Y  A  P  I  J  S  C  Q
H  S  W  W  S  A  N  E  R  V  P  K  V  E  T  Z  F
V  C  T  K  I  R  S  R  L  O  P  I  I  E  C  P  K
H  A  L  L  O  W  E  E  N  M  L  K  N  A  R  Z  H
I  R  O  C  I  B  X  F  U  J  E  A  G  Q  B  Q  P
T  F  A  K  N  H  H  P  L  L  C  N  G  W  Z  F  E
S  W  E  A  T  E  R  B  U  E  P  W  A  G  B  U  S
H  A  R  V  E  S  T  Z  P  R  O  D  Y  L  D  K  M
Q  C  J  G  H  T  X  F  X  D  T  W  K  Y  R  P  O
```

FALL

AUTUMN, HARVEST, LEAVES, PUMPKIN, APPLE, SWEATER, BONFIRE, HAY RIDE, ACORN, SCARF, HALLOWEEN, THANKSGIVING, CIDER, HARVEST, CORNUCOPIA, FOLIAGE, PECAN, CRANBERRY, SOUP, HARVEST

# WORD SEARCH #3

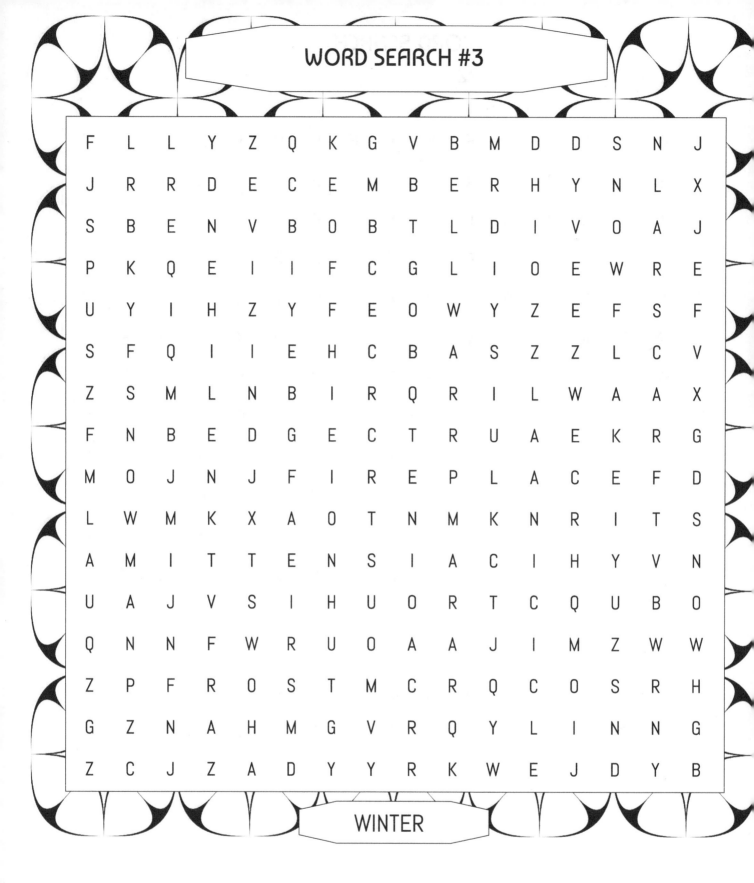

```
F  L  L  Y  Z  Q  K  G  V  B  M  D  D  S  N  J
J  R  R  D  E  C  E  M  B  E  R  H  Y  N  L  X
S  B  E  N  V  B  O  B  T  L  D  I  V  O  A  J
P  K  Q  E  I  I  F  C  G  L  I  O  E  W  R  E
U  Y  I  H  Z  Y  F  E  O  W  Y  Z  E  F  S  F
S  F  Q  I  I  E  H  C  B  A  S  Z  Z  L  C  V
Z  S  M  L  N  B  I  R  Q  R  I  L  W  A  A  X
F  N  B  E  D  G  E  C  T  R  U  A  E  K  R  G
M  O  J  N  J  F  I  R  E  P  L  A  C  E  F  D
L  W  M  K  X  A  O  T  N  M  K  N  R  I  T  S
A  M  I  T  T  E  N  S  I  A  C  I  H  Y  V  N
U  A  J  V  S  I  H  U  O  R  T  C  Q  U  B  O
Q  N  N  F  W  R  U  O  A  A  J  I  M  Z  W  W
Z  P  F  R  O  S  T  M  C  R  Q  C  O  S  R  H
G  Z  N  A  H  M  G  V  R  Q  Y  L  I  N  N  G
Z  C  J  Z  A  D  Y  Y  R  K  W  E  J  D  Y  B
```

WINTER

SNOW, COLD, ICE, FROST, FREEZE, BLIZZARD, SLEET, HIBERNATION, MITTENS, SCARF, FIRE PLACE, COCOA, WINTERIZE, SNOWFLAKE, ICICLE, SNOW MAN, DECEMBER, JANUARY, FEBRUARY, SKIING

# WORD SEARCH #4

```
W  H  S  L  C  V  N  B  L  O  S  S  O  M  U  G  T  V
A  Y  P  X  A  H  M  Q  V  B  G  L  K  A  E  U  R  G
R  W  I  S  Y  P  E  E  F  J  U  H  I  Y  B  U  F  M
M  E  C  O  N  H  R  R  J  S  Z  Z  E  N  R  R  F  D
T  D  N  Y  L  Y  B  I  R  Y  A  E  D  N  W  T  W  D
H  F  I  E  N  U  W  A  L  Y  F  R  A  I  N  K  B  W
K  L  C  L  W  S  Z  F  R  D  B  L  F  B  G  X  D  R
L  O  I  S  T  A  R  F  A  L  L  L  F  W  V  B  C  T
H  W  I  C  U  E  L  G  Z  E  S  J  O  X  O  P  E  B
Z  E  Y  C  T  N  A  G  R  A  S  S  D  S  V  C  A  F
N  R  T  T  L  P  S  B  R  Q  X  P  I  W  S  A  B  B
S  S  U  S  P  C  M  H  X  O  C  W  L  Y  T  O  H  P
P  B  L  Q  E  U  R  A  I  N  B  O  W  M  Z  I  M  I
R  Q  I  A  Q  A  A  X  W  N  W  I  E  U  B  Z  U  Z
O  A  P  L  D  L  S  F  Y  G  E  E  N  D  L  U  O  F
U  U  H  C  Q  A  A  T  A  F  F  P  X  J  N  M  X  W
T  I  G  C  V  C  H  T  E  A  P  I  D  M  A  R  U  F
I  E  A  T  E  I  V  G  A  R  D  E  N  I  N  G  I  T
```

SPRING

BLOSSOM, FLOWERS, SUNSHINE, RAIN, BUTTERFLY, PICNIC, GARDENING, APRIL, MAY, TULIP, CHERRY BLOSSOM, DAFFODIL, EASTER, GRASS, RAINBOW, ROBIN, SPROUT, UMBRELLA, WARMTH, RENEWAL

# WORD SEARCH #5

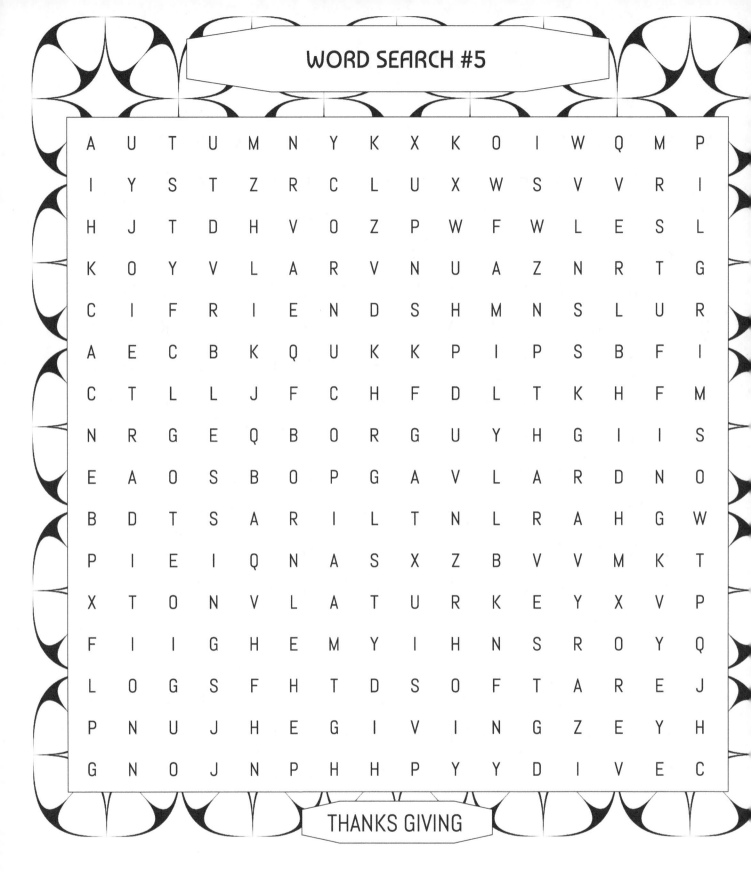

```
A U T U M N Y K X K O I W Q M P
I Y S T Z R C L U X W S V V R I
H J T D H V O Z P W F W L E S L
K O Y V L A R V N U A Z N R T G
C I F R I E N D S H M N S L U R
A E C B K Q U K K P I P S B F I
C T L L J F C H F D L T K H F M
N R G E Q B O R G U Y H G I I S
E A O S B P G A V L A R D N O
B D T S A R I L T N L R A H G W
P I E I Q N A S X Z B V V M K T
X T O N V L A T U R K E Y X V P
F I I G H E M Y I H N S R O Y Q
L O G S F H T D S O F T A R E J
P N U J H E G I V I N G Z E Y H
G N O J N P H H P Y Y D I V E C
```

THANKS GIVING

TURKEY, GRAVY, FEAST, PILGRIMS, NATIVE, HARVEST, FAMILY, FRIENDS, STUFFING, PUMPKIN, CRANBERRY, CORNUCOPIA, BLESSINGS, AUTUMN, PIE, THANKFUL, TRADITION, CELEBRATION, DINNER, GIVING

# WORD SEARCH #6

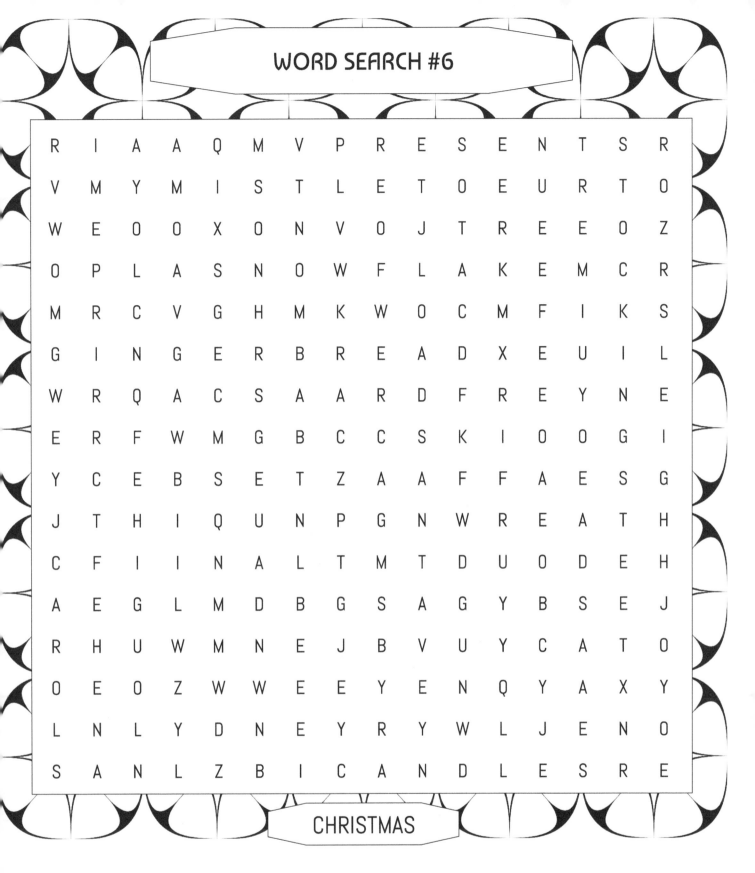

```
R  I  A  A  Q  M  V  P  R  E  S  E  N  T  S  R
V  M  Y  M  I  S  T  L  E  T  O  E  U  R  T  O
W  E  O  O  X  O  N  V  O  J  T  R  E  E  O  Z
O  P  L  A  S  N  O  W  F  L  A  K  E  M  C  R
M  R  C  V  G  H  M  K  W  O  C  M  F  I  K  S
G  I  N  G  E  R  B  R  E  A  D  X  E  U  I  L
W  R  Q  A  C  S  A  A  R  D  F  R  E  Y  N  E
E  R  F  W  M  G  B  C  C  S  K  I  O  O  G  I
Y  C  E  B  S  E  T  Z  A  A  F  F  A  E  S  G
J  T  H  I  Q  U  N  P  G  N  W  R  E  A  T  H
C  F  I  I  N  A  L  T  M  T  D  U  O  D  E  H
A  E  G  L  M  D  B  G  S  A  G  Y  B  S  E  J
R  H  U  W  M  N  E  J  B  V  U  Y  C  A  T  O
O  E  O  Z  W  W  E  E  Y  E  N  Q  Y  A  X  Y
L  N  L  Y  D  N  E  Y  R  Y  W  L  J  E  N  O
S  A  N  L  Z  B  I  C  A  N  D  L  E  S  R  E
```

CHRISTMAS

SANTA, PRESENTS, TREE, ORNAMENTS, REINDEER, SLEIGH, SNOW FLAKE, MISTLETOE, SNOWMAN, STOCKINGS, WREATH, CANDLES, CAROLS, GINGER BREAD, NUT CRACKER, CHIMNEY, ELVES, CANDY CANE, FROSTY, JOY

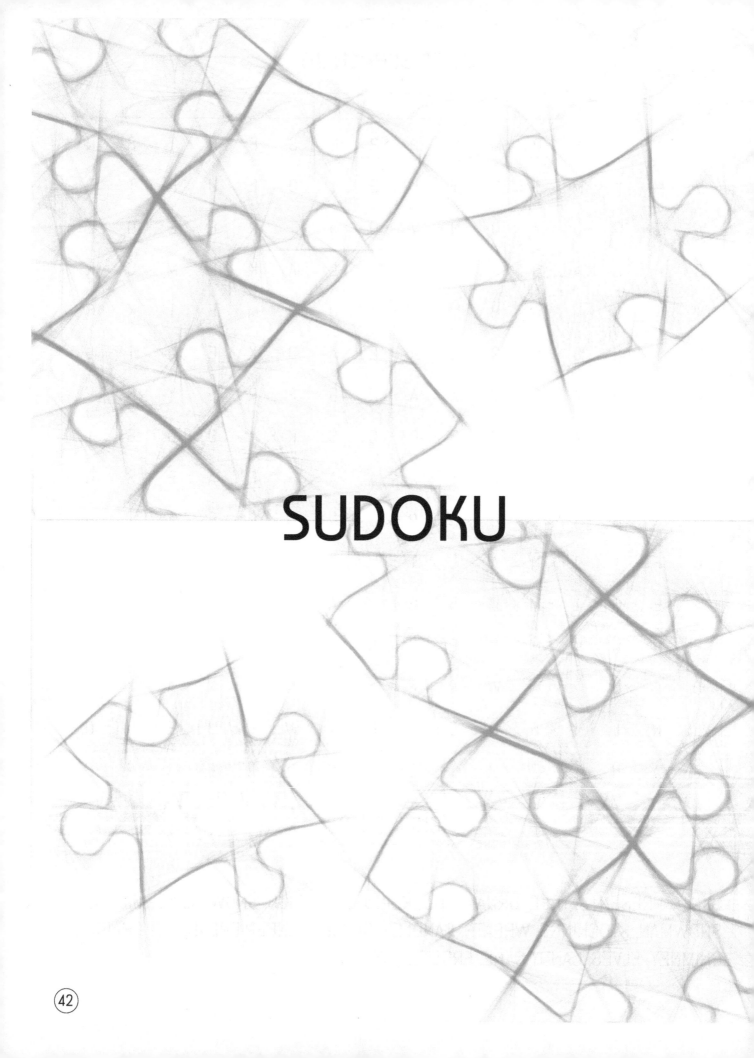

# SUDOKU

# SUDOKU

SUDOKU IS A LOGIC BASED NUMBER PLACEMENT PUZZLE.

HOW TO PLAY:
FILL UP THE EMPTY GRIDS WITH NUMBERS 1-9 SUCH THAT EVERY 9 ROW, EVERY 9 COLUMN AND EVERY 3X3 GRID HAS NUMBERS 1-9 WITHOUT REPETITION.
THE PUZZLE IS SOLVED WHEN THE ENTIRE GRID IS FILLED WITH NUMBERS ACCORDING TO THE RULES

TIPS:
START WITH ROWS, COLUMNS OR SUBGRIDS WITH ONLY A FEW MISSING NUMBERS AND TRY TO FILL THEM IN

EXAMPLE:

| 4 | 1 | 9 | 6 | 2 | 8 |   | 5 | 7 |
|---|---|---|---|---|---|---|---|---|
| 5 | 6 | 2 | 1 | 7 | 3 | 9 | 8 | 4 |
| 8 | 3 | 7 | 9 | 5 | 4 | 6 | 2 | 1 |
| 9 | 4 | 3 | 7 | 6 | 5 | 2 | 1 | 8 |
| 1 | 5 | 6 | 8 | 4 | 2 | 7 | 9 | 3 |
| 2 | 7 | 8 | 3 | 1 |   |   | 6 | 5 |
|   | 9 | 4 | 5 | 3 | 1 |   | 7 | 2 |
| 7 | 2 | 5 | 4 | 8 | 6 | 1 | 3 | 9 |
| 3 | 8 | 1 | 2 | 9 | 7 | 5 | 4 | 6 |

**A**

| 4 | 1 | 9 | 6 | 2 | 8 | *3* | 5 | 7 |
|---|---|---|---|---|---|---|---|---|
| 5 | 6 | 2 | 1 | 7 | 3 | 9 | 8 | 4 |
| 8 | 3 | 7 | 9 | 5 | 4 | 6 | 2 | 1 |
| 9 | 4 | 3 | 7 | 6 | 5 | 2 | 1 | 8 |
| 1 | 5 | 6 | 8 | 4 | 2 | 7 | 9 | 3 |
| 2 | 7 | 8 | 3 | 1 | *9* |   | 6 | 5 |
| *6* | 9 | 4 | 5 | 3 | 1 |   | 7 | 2 |
| 7 | 2 | 5 | 4 | 8 | 6 | 1 | 3 | 9 |
| 3 | 8 | 1 | 2 | 9 | 7 | 5 | 4 | 6 |

**B**     **C**

1. CONSIDERING ROW A, IT HAS ALL NUMBERS FROM 1 TO 9 EXCEPT 3. THE EMPTY CELL IS SOLVED WITH NUMBER 3
2. CONSIDERING COLUMN B, IT HAS ALL NUMBERS FROM 1 TO 9 EXCEPT 6. THE EMPTY CELL IS SOLVED WITH NUMBER 6
3. CONSIDERING SUB-GRID C, IT HAS ALL NUMBERS FROM 1 TO 9 EXCEPT 9. THE EMPTY CELL IS SOLVED WITH NUMBER 9

# SUDOKU

**#1**

**#2**

**DIFFICULTY LEVEL VERY EASY**

## #1

| 9 |   |   |   |   |   |   |   |   |
|---|---|---|---|---|---|---|---|---|
| 1 |   | 7 |   |   | 3 | 8 | 2 |   |
|   | 2 | 5 |   | 8 | 7 | 9 |   |   |
| 8 | 5 | 1 | 3 | 6 | 4 | 7 |   | 2 |
| 7 |   | 3 | 5 | 2 | 9 | 1 |   | 8 |
|   |   |   | 7 | 1 |   | 5 |   | 6 |
|   | 3 |   | 4 |   |   | 6 | 1 |   |
|   |   |   | 8 | 3 |   |   |   |   |
|   | 7 | 4 |   |   | 1 | 2 | 8 | 3 |

## #2

| 6 | 8 | 9 |   | 7 | 1 |   | 4 | 3 |
|---|---|---|---|---|---|---|---|---|
| 5 |   | 1 |   | 4 |   | 7 |   | 9 |
| 7 | 4 | 3 | 5 |   |   | 2 | 1 | 8 |
|   |   |   | 7 | 5 |   |   | 2 |   |
| 2 |   |   | 4 | 1 | 8 | 9 |   |   |
| 1 | 5 | 6 | 9 |   | 2 |   |   |   |
| 3 | 7 |   | 1 | 8 | 4 |   | 9 | 2 |
| 8 |   |   |   | 9 |   | 4 | 3 | 5 |
|   | 6 |   | 3 | 2 |   |   |   | 7 |

## #3

| 1 | 9 | 5 |   |   | 6 |   | 7 |   |
|---|---|---|---|---|---|---|---|---|
|   | 1 |   |   | 7 |   |   | 2 |   |
|   |   |   | 8 | 2 |   |   | 1 |   |
| 8 |   |   | 4 |   | 9 |   |   | 7 |
|   |   | 9 | 7 |   |   | 1 |   |   |
| 4 | 7 | 1 |   | 5 |   | 8 | 6 |   |
| 1 | 8 |   | 6 |   | 7 | 5 | 3 |   |
|   | 5 |   | 2 |   | 4 |   | 8 | 1 |
| 3 |   | 6 | 5 | 8 | 1 | 7 |   | 2 |

## #4

|   |   |   | 4 | 7 | 2 | 1 |   |   |
|---|---|---|---|---|---|---|---|---|
|   | 1 |   |   | 6 |   |   |   | 7 |
| 2 |   |   |   | 8 | 9 |   | 5 |   |
| 9 |   |   | 8 |   | 3 |   | 1 | 4 |
| 1 |   | 6 | 9 | 5 |   | 7 | 2 | 3 |
| 3 |   | 2 | 6 |   |   | 9 | 8 |   |
| 6 | 9 | 5 |   |   |   |   | 3 | 2 |
|   |   | 8 |   |   |   | 5 |   | 1 |
|   |   | 1 |   |   | 8 |   |   | 9 |

**#5**

| | | | 3 | 4 | 7 | 9 | | |
|---|---|---|---|---|---|---|---|---|
| 1 | 7 | 9 | | | | | | 2 |
| | | 6 | 9 | 2 | | | | 8 |
| 3 | 1 | | 6 | 8 | | | | |
| 6 | | | | | | 4 | | |
| | | 5 | 1 | | 3 | | | 7 |
| | 5 | 1 | | 7 | | | | 9 |
| 7 | 9 | 3 | 2 | 5 | | | 8 | 4 |
| 2 | 6 | 4 | 1 | 9 | 8 | 7 | 5 | |

**#6**

| 5 | | | | 4 | | 1 | | 3 |
|---|---|---|---|---|---|---|---|---|
| 2 | 4 | 7 | | 3 | 1 | 8 | | |
| | | | | | 6 | 7 | | 4 |
| | | 8 | | | | | | 1 |
| | | 3 | 8 | 9 | 2 | | | 7 |
| | | 4 | 1 | 7 | | 9 | | |
| | | | 8 | 7 | | | | |
| 7 | | | 3 | 1 | 5 | 4 | 8 | |
| | 1 | 5 | 4 | | | 9 | 2 | |

**#7**

| | 1 | | 8 | | 4 | 3 | 9 | |
|---|---|---|---|---|---|---|---|---|
| 2 | 3 | 4 | | | 9 | | 1 | |
| 8 | | 9 | | | | 4 | | 7 |
| | | 8 | 4 | | 5 | 2 | | |
| | | | 6 | | | 7 | 9 | |
| | 2 | | | | | | | 4 |
| | | | | 8 | | 4 | | |
| | 7 | 1 | 2 | 4 | | 5 | 8 | 6 |
| | 8 | | 5 | | 6 | 9 | 3 | 1 |

**#8**

| 1 | | | | 2 | | | | 8 |
|---|---|---|---|---|---|---|---|---|
| 8 | | 5 | | | | | | 6 |
| | | | 8 | | | 7 | | 3 |
| | 4 | 1 | | | | 6 | | 7 |
| | | | | 7 | | 8 | 9 | |
| 8 | 7 | 9 | 6 | 3 | | 4 | 5 | 1 |
| 6 | | | | 4 | 8 | | | |
| 7 | | | 1 | | | 2 | | |
| 3 | | | 7 | 9 | | 1 | | |

# SUDOKU

**#9**

| | | 9 | 7 | | | | 1 | 6 |
|---|---|---|---|---|---|---|---|---|
| | 3 | | | 5 | 9 | 4 | | |
| 1 | | 4 | | 9 | | 7 | 3 | |
| 3 | 7 | | 4 | | | 5 | 9 | |
| | | | 8 | | | | | |
| 5 | 2 | 6 | 3 | | | | | |
| | 6 | | | 4 | | | | |
| 7 | | 3 | 2 | 8 | | | 5 | |
| | | 3 | | 6 | | | | |

**#10**

| | | | | 8 | 6 | 7 | | |
|---|---|---|---|---|---|---|---|---|
| | | | | | | | 1 | 8 |
| | | | | | 9 | 4 | | |
| | 6 | | | | 4 | 1 | | |
| | 9 | | 8 | | | 2 | 6 | |
| 2 | | 3 | 7 | 6 | 1 | | 4 | |
| 9 | 3 | 8 | 6 | 4 | 2 | | | |
| 5 | | 9 | | 3 | | | | |
| | | | | 8 | | 3 | | |

**#11**

| | | | | | 4 | 1 | | |
|---|---|---|---|---|---|---|---|---|
| | | 6 | | 4 | 2 | 8 | 5 | |
| | | 1 | | | | | | |
| 4 | | 2 | 8 | | 5 | 7 | 1 | |
| | 8 | | | 7 | 9 | | | |
| | | 2 | | 3 | | | | |
| 2 | | 8 | 7 | | | | 3 | |
| 7 | 1 | 4 | | 8 | | 5 | | |
| 3 | | 6 | 5 | 2 | | 4 | | 8 |

**#12**

| | 9 | | | | | | | |
|---|---|---|---|---|---|---|---|---|
| 1 | | 3 | 8 | | 2 | | | |
| 2 | | 7 | | | | | 1 | 6 |
| 7 | 3 | 5 | | | | 9 | 6 | |
| | 1 | 6 | 3 | | | 7 | | 2 |
| | | 6 | 7 | | | 1 | 3 | 5 |
| | 1 | | | | | | | |
| 6 | 2 | 8 | | 5 | 3 | | 7 | 1 |
| | 9 | 4 | | | 7 | 3 | | |

## DIFFICULTY LEVEL
### EASY

#13

| | 16 | | | | 10 | | 15 | 13 | 5 | 4 | | | | 3 | |
|---|---|---|---|---|---|---|---|---|---|---|---|---|---|---|---|
| 6 | 15 | | 4 | 14 | | 9 | | 1 | | 3 | | 7 | | | |
| 2 | | 5 | 7 | | | | | 10 | | 16 | 9 | | | | |
| | | 9 | 12 | | 2 | | 4 | 6 | | | | | | | 13 |
| | | | | | | 2 | | 16 | | | 12 | 11 | 8 | 14 | 4 |
| | | | | | 1 | | | | 6 | 14 | | | | | 5 |
| | | | 9 | 16 | | 7 | | | | 8 | | 10 | 13 | 1 | 6 |
| 15 | 14 | | | | 4 | 8 | | | 11 | 1 | | | 7 | 16 | 12 |
| 3 | | | | 9 | | | | | | 13 | | 4 | | 10 | 16 |
| | | | | | | 4 | 6 | | | | 11 | | | 5 | 7 |
| | 12 | 6 | | 2 | 13 | | | 14 | 10 | 5 | | | 11 | | |
| 13 | | | | | | | | | | | | 14 | 6 | | 2 |
| 5 | | | | 4 | 7 | 12 | 11 | 8 | | | 15 | | | | |
| | 1 | | | | 6 | | | | | | 13 | | | | |
| | 11 | | 3 | 15 | 14 | 13 | 2 | | 4 | | | 8 | 16 | | |
| | | | | 8 | 9 | 1 | 10 | | | | 3 | | 4 | | |

DIFFICULTY LEVEL
EASY

16 X 16

# SUDOKU

**#14**
```
6 5 3 | . . . | . 8 .
3 . 7 | . . . | . 2 .
4 7 2 | 5 . . | 3 . .
------+-------+------
6 1 . | . . . | 4 . .
. . . | 8 . . | 6 . .
. 8 6 | 7 . 2 | . . .
------+-------+------
. 6 1 | . . . | 8 4 .
8 . . | . 7 6 | . . .
7 . 8 | . . . | 1 3 .
```

**#15**
```
. . 9 | . . . | . . 1
. 6 . | . 7 . | 2 5 .
. . . | . . 1 | 8 . .
------+-------+------
. . 5 | . . . | 9 8 7
4 5 8 | . . 9 | . . .
9 . . | 8 1 . | . 2 5
------+-------+------
. . . | 2 3 6 | . . .
. . . | . . . | . . .
1 . . | . . . | 7 . 4
```

**#16**
```
. 3 . | 4 9 . | 8 . 6
8 . 6 | . . 7 | . . .
4 9 . | 8 . . | 2 . .
------+-------+------
1 7 4 | . . . | 3 . .
. . . | 6 3 . | . . .
9 . . | . . . | . . 8
------+-------+------
. 5 9 | . . . | . . 1
. . . | 3 5 4 | . 6 2
. . . | . 2 . | 7 . .
```

**#17**
```
. . 4 | 2 . 3 | . . 1
6 8 1 | . . . | . 4 .
. 2 3 | . . . | . . .
------+-------+------
. . 8 | . . 1 | 9 . .
7 . . | 8 6 . | 1 . .
. . . | 7 . . | 4 . .
------+-------+------
. 3 9 | 6 . . | 7 . .
. . . | 4 . 5 | 2 1 .
. . . | 3 . . | 6 . .
```

DIFFICULTY LEVEL
NORMAL

| | | | | | | | | | | | | | | | |
|---|---|---|---|---|---|---|---|---|---|---|---|---|---|---|---|
| 8 | | | | | | | | 15 | | | | 3 | 6 | 13 | |
| 10 | | 13 | 16 | | 8 | | | 1 | | | | | | | |
| | | 14 | 15 | 13 | 5 | | | | | | | | 2 | 12 | |
| | 3 | | 4 | 15 | 9 | | | | | | | | 16 | 8 | |
| | | | 13 | | 3 | | | 9 | 11 | | 7 | | 1 | 2 | 6 |
| | | | 11 | | 6 | | | | | | 1 | | | | |
| 5 | | | | | 9 | | | | | | | 4 | 13 | 14 | |
| | 4 | | | 15 | | 10 | 14 | | | 8 | | | | | |
| | | 1 | 3 | | | | | | | 4 | | | | 5 | 13 |
| | | | | | 15 | | | 1 | 9 | 6 | 12 | | | | |
| 12 | | 4 | | 13 | | | | 8 | 14 | 2 | | 10 | | | |
| 15 | 14 | | | | | | | | | | | 2 | | | |
| | | 12 | | | 9 | 14 | | | | 1 | | | 4 | 3 | 5 |
| | 16 | | 10 | | | | | | | | | | | | |
| | | | | | | | | | | | | 12 | | | |
| | | | | | 16 | | | 8 | | | | | | | |

**#19**

| | | | | | | | | |
|---|---|---|---|---|---|---|---|---|
| 7 | | | | | 1 | | | |
| | | 4 | 8 | | 6 | | | 7 |
| 2 | | | 9 | | | 4 | | |
| | | | 8 | | | 5 | 4 | |
| 1 | | | 5 | | | | 6 | |
| | | | | 7 | 9 | | 3 | |
| | 8 | | 3 | 5 | 2 | 7 | | |
| | | | | 8 | | | | |
| | 6 | | | 9 | 1 | | | |

**#20**

| | | | | | | | | |
|---|---|---|---|---|---|---|---|---|
| | | | 3 | 6 | 8 | 7 | | |
| 4 | 2 | 7 | | 9 | | | 6 | |
| 3 | | | | | | | 9 | |
| | | | | | | 3 | 1 | |
| 6 | | | | | 7 | | | |
| | | | 4 | | | 2 | | |
| 7 | 5 | | 9 | | | | | |
| | 6 | 8 | | 3 | | | | 5 |
| 1 | | | 5 | | | | 3 | 7 |

**#21**

| | | | | | | | | |
|---|---|---|---|---|---|---|---|---|
| 4 | 2 | 6 | | 7 | 3 | 1 | 5 | |
| | 8 | | | | | | 4 | |
| | 5 | | 3 | | | | 7 | |
| | | | 3 | 9 | | | | |
| | | 3 | | | | 7 | 4 | |
| 6 | | | | | | | | |
| 2 | 1 | | 8 | | | 3 | | |
| 5 | | | | 6 | 1 | | | |
| | 6 | | 1 | | 4 | | | |

**#22**

| | | | | | | | | |
|---|---|---|---|---|---|---|---|---|
| | | | | | 7 | | 1 | 3 |
| 7 | 8 | | | | 1 | | 4 | 2 |
| | 6 | | | | | | 7 | |
| | | 2 | 4 | | | | | 7 |
| 8 | 4 | | 2 | | | 6 | 1 | 9 |
| | | | 1 | | | 4 | | 6 |
| 3 | | | 4 | 9 | | 8 | | |
| | | | 7 | | 8 | | 9 | |
| | | | 1 | | | 6 | | |

DIFFICULTY LEVEL
MEDIUM

# SUDOKU

**DIFFICULTY LEVEL HARD**

## #23

|   |   |   |   |   |   |   |   |   |
|---|---|---|---|---|---|---|---|---|
|   | 8 |   | 3 |   | 1 | 4 |   |   |
| 4 | 1 | 6 | 8 |   | 5 |   |   |   |
|   | 3 |   | 7 | 6 | 2 |   |   |   |
| 3 |   | 4 | 7 |   | 8 | 9 | 6 |   |
|   |   |   |   | 3 |   |   |   |   |
| 8 |   |   | 9 |   | 2 | 7 |   |   |
|   |   |   |   |   |   |   |   |   |
|   | 7 |   | 6 | 4 |   | 8 |   |   |
| 2 |   |   | 3 | 9 |   | 4 |   |   |

## #24

|   |   |   |   |   |   |   |   |   |
|---|---|---|---|---|---|---|---|---|
|   |   |   |   |   | 3 |   | 6 |   |
| 6 |   |   |   | 5 |   | 9 |   | 4 |
| 8 |   |   |   |   |   | 2 | 5 |   |
|   | 1 | 8 |   |   | 4 |   | 3 |   |
| 4 |   |   | 1 |   |   | 7 |   |   |
| 5 |   | 3 |   |   |   | 4 |   |   |
|   |   |   | 2 | 8 | 9 |   |   |   |
|   | 5 |   |   | 4 |   |   |   |   |
|   |   |   |   | 7 | 1 |   |   |   |

## #25

|   |   |   |   |   |   |   |   |   |
|---|---|---|---|---|---|---|---|---|
| 2 |   |   |   | 8 | 7 | 6 |   |   |
|   |   |   | 6 |   |   |   | 9 |   |
|   |   |   |   |   | 1 |   |   |   |
| 6 |   |   |   | 3 |   | 5 |   |   |
|   | 9 | 3 | 8 |   | 2 | 1 |   |   |
|   |   |   | 3 |   | 8 |   |   |   |
| 8 |   | 7 | 4 | 9 |   |   |   |   |
|   | 1 | 5 |   |   |   |   |   |   |
|   | 2 | 9 |   |   | 6 |   |   |   |

## #26

|   |   |   |   |   |   |   |   |   |
|---|---|---|---|---|---|---|---|---|
|   |   |   |   |   | 2 |   | 9 | 5 |
|   |   |   |   | 1 |   | 7 |   |   |
| 9 | 3 | 4 |   |   |   | 7 | 8 |   |
|   |   |   |   |   |   | 4 |   |   |
| 4 | 5 |   | 2 |   |   |   |   | 9 |
| 7 |   |   |   |   |   |   |   |   |
| 2 |   |   |   | 4 |   |   | 6 | 1 |
|   |   |   |   | 8 |   |   |   | 7 |
|   |   |   |   | 7 |   | 6 | 9 |   |

# SUDOKU - FUN FACTS

1. THE 9X9 FORMAT IS THE MOST POPULAR AND IS CALLED THE CLASSIC SUDOKU

2. THE INITIAL VERSIONS WERE MERE MAGIC SQUARES WITH MISSING NUMBERS AND WERE PUBLISHED WITH A DIFFERENT NAME - "NUMBER PLACE" IN A FRENCH DAILY

3. THE TODAY'S VERSION OF THE GAME WAS PUBLISHED WITH THE NAME "SUDOKU" IN 1986 BY A JAPANESE PUZZLE COMPANY

4. THE POPULAR VARIANT - "KILLER SUDOKU" COMBINES SUDOKU WITH KAKURO

5. SINCE 2006, SUDOKU HAS BEEN INCLUDED IN THE WORLD PUZZLE CHAMPIONSHIP

6. IN 2012, DURING THE "SUDOKU COMBAT" EVENT IN CHINA, 2220 PARTICIPANTS SET THE GUINNESS WORLD RECORD FOR THE LARGEST NUMBER OF PEOPLE PLAYING SUDOKU SIMULTANEOUSLY

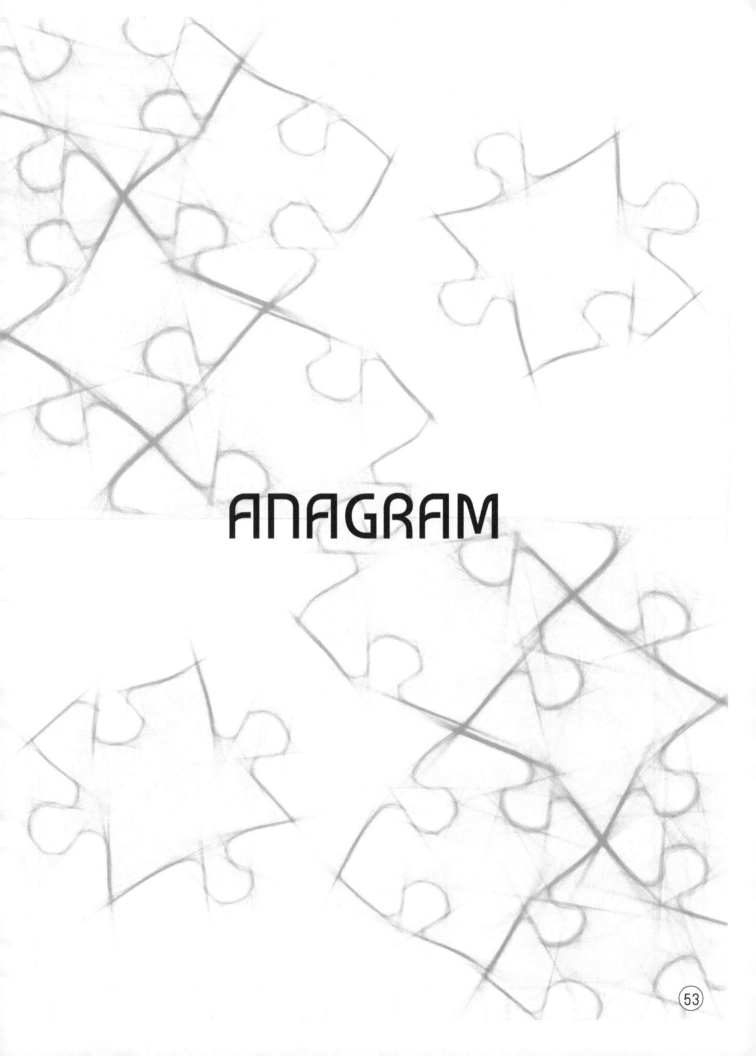

# ANAGRAM

# ANAGRAM #1

| | | | |
|---|---|---|---|
| LPEPA | = _____ | HICRA | = _____ |
| ANECD | = _____ | LGIHT | = _____ |
| LMEIS | = _____ | NCEOA | = _____ |
| BCHAE | = _____ | CULOD | = _____ |
| PAHYP | = _____ | HNCLU | = _____ |
| ESHOU | = _____ | UMICS | = _____ |
| EGRIT | = _____ | NLAPT | = _____ |
| AEWRT | = _____ | BIRTBA | = _____ |
| ELMNO | = _____ | CLCOK | = _____ |
| RBADE | = _____ | OHSER | = _____ |
| AROCTR | = _____ | RSTSA | = _____ |
| OBSKO | = _____ | MYOEN | = _____ |
| YLLEJ | = _____ | ELISD | = _____ |
| MEAPL | = _____ | TWEES | = _____ |
| LTABE | = _____ | TNAIP | = _____ |
| RASSG | = _____ | GTIHN | = _____ |
| URCTK | = _____ | EUNEQ | = _____ |
| RRIVE | = _____ | OUSEM | = _____ |
| TUIEQ | = _____ | RAHET | = _____ |
| SILNA | = _____ | ABSEN | = _____ |
| HCPAE | = _____ | ESDSR | = _____ |
| GAELN | = _____ | INWSG | = _____ |
| OHESS | = _____ | JIECU | = _____ |
| HLSEL | = _____ | SYNUN | = _____ |
| GMNOA | = _____ | DCANY | = _____ |
| GSAERP | = _____ | APPRE | = _____ |
| RAHET | = _____ | ZIAPZ | = _____ |
| YRTOS | = _____ | HTWCA | = _____ |
| NKESA | = _____ | DLCHI | = _____ |
| LRAIT | = _____ | YEALF | = _____ |

# ANAGRAM #2

| | | | |
|---|---|---|---|
| ZBEREE | = _____ | TUERBT | = _____ |
| MCAAER | = _____ | DCLAEN | = _____ |
| EOEFFC | = _____ | CIEOKO | = _____ |
| ODCORT | = _____ | LRLDOA | = _____ |
| ERWFOL | = _____ | IUARGT | = _____ |
| MEARHM | = _____ | CAKETJ | = _____ |
| NLUJEG | = _____ | TTRELE | = _____ |
| ORIMRR | = _____ | EGRONA | = _____ |
| EPLICN | = _____ | OERTKC | = _____ |
| LRESVI | = _____ | OSEKCT | = _____ |
| KTECIT | = _____ | MELUBALR | = _____ |
| WWIDNO | = _____ | ANAANB | = _____ |
| BOLTET | = _____ | RYEHRC | = _____ |
| ECRCLI | = _____ | EGDANR | = _____ |
| EDRNNI | = _____ | INEENG | = _____ |
| YLMFAI | = _____ | ERGAND | = _____ |
| GREPSA | = _____ | GOISLO | = _____ |
| ETICNS | = _____ | WJEEL | = _____ |
| JWIGAS | = _____ | ALDRDE | = _____ |
| PPOATL | = _____ | ONELM | = _____ |

# ANAGRAM #3

| | | | |
|---|---|---|---|
| ARLDIZ | = _____ | PMLAE | = _____ |
| UMIFNF | = _____ | ONNTAI | = _____ |
| EEDLEN | = _____ | IOFECF | = _____ |
| OVILE | = _____ | PCAALE | = _____ |
| PTAORR | = _____ | BLPBEE | = _____ |
| EOPTKC | = _____ | BIBRAT | = _____ |
| IARWOBN | = _____ | RLLREO | = _____ |
| SNMOLA | = _____ | EAGSAUS | = _____ |
| SWHAOD | = _____ | SARHK | = _____ |
| IRSENG | = _____ | RCCSOE | = _____ |
| RITPIS | = _____ | RASSIT | = _____ |
| OMTTOA | = _____ | RUTTLE | = _____ |
| VEEVTL | = _____ | LESEVS | = _____ |
| LAWETL | = _____ | SEWRHA | = _____ |
| TWOBAM | = _____ | IRTWER | = _____ |
| LLWYEO | = _____ | IPEZPR | = _____ |
| OASRNC | = _____ | ARTSTI | = _____ |
| VBREEA | = _____ | TACLES | = _____ |
| CUSICR | = _____ | CISKEOO | = _____ |
| UDANMID | = _____ | HMEULI | = _____ |

# ANAGRAM #4

| | | | |
|---|---|---|---|
| AYSBS | = _____ | TUEAC | = _____ |
| AEGLI | = _____ | AAJR | = _____ |
| ELPMA | = _____ | GYARN | = _____ |
| IRAD | = _____ | ESANTC | = _____ |
| ERAUG | = _____ | BLVEE | = _____ |
| BANLD | = _____ | BLNUT | = _____ |
| BIKRS | = _____ | DOBRO | = _____ |
| UNACJ | = _____ | CAPRE | = _____ |
| HCOAS | = _____ | CLTEF | = _____ |
| EOVCL | = _____ | GCNLU | = _____ |
| XAOC | = _____ | RISPC | = _____ |
| MBRCU | = _____ | SCUTR | = _____ |
| IPCUD | = _____ | YNICC | = _____ |
| DNDYA | = _____ | TUDNA | = _____ |
| DCYOE | = _____ | URMDE | = _____ |
| IRDVE | = _____ | TDFRA | = _____ |
| DTFRI | = _____ | OLLRD | = _____ |
| ENDOR | = _____ | ECITD | = _____ |
| OVEEK | = _____ | LTEXA | = _____ |
| TNAFI | = _____ | KFLCI | = _____ |
| FUKEL | = _____ | LYOFL | = _____ |
| OFAYR | = _____ | UEFGD | = _____ |
| NIFGU | = _____ | IDDGY | = _____ |
| TLGNI | = _____ | OOLMG | = _____ |
| FRGUF | = _____ | HEATS | = _____ |
| NIHGE | = _____ | ODHAR | = _____ |
| HNAYE | = _____ | CICLIE | = _____ |
| LOGIO | = _____ | BMIUE | = _____ |
| AENIN | = _____ | NTRIE | = _____ |
| IUXFLN | = _____ | UNAJT | = _____ |

# SQUARE SUM

# SQUARE SUM

## #1

| | + | | / | | 6 |
|---|---|---|---|---|---|
| + | ■ | + | ■ | + | |
| | − | | X | | 40 |
| X | ■ | + | ■ | X | |
| | + | | − | | 2 |
| 45 | | 14 | | 70 | |

## #3

| | + | | X | | 126 |
|---|---|---|---|---|---|
| − | ■ | + | ■ | + | |
| | + | | − | | 5 |
| + | ■ | X | ■ | + | |
| | + | | X | | 20 |
| 2 | | 24 | | 18 | |

## #2

| | − | | X | | 5 |
|---|---|---|---|---|---|
| + | ■ | + | ■ | + | |
| | − | | − | | 3 |
| − | ■ | X | ■ | / | |
| | + | | X | | 119 |
| 2 | | 36 | | 1 | |

## #4

| | + | | + | | 14 |
|---|---|---|---|---|---|
| + | ■ | + | ■ | + | |
| | + | | X | | 20 |
| − | ■ | X | ■ | − | |
| | + | | + | | 19 |
| 2 | | 77 | | 1 | |

# SQUARE SUM

## #5

| | + | | X | | **34** |
|---|---|---|---|---|---|
| + | ⬛ | + | ⬛ | + | |
| | − | | + | | **7** |
| + | ⬛ | X | ⬛ | X | |
| | − | | X | | **70** |
| **18** | | **54** | | **35** | |

## #7

| | + | | X | | **42** |
|---|---|---|---|---|---|
| − | ⬛ | + | ⬛ | + | |
| | + | | X | | **28** |
| X | ⬛ | / | ⬛ | X | |
| | + | | + | | **21** |
| **8** | | **12** | | **117** | |

## #6

| | − | | X | | **24** |
|---|---|---|---|---|---|
| + | ⬛ | + | ⬛ | + | |
| | − | | X | | **39** |
| X | ⬛ | + | ⬛ | X | |
| | − | | − | | **1** |
| **135** | | **12** | | **14** | |

## #8

| | + | | X | | **108** |
|---|---|---|---|---|---|
| + | ⬛ | + | ⬛ | − | |
| | + | | − | | **5** |
| / | ⬛ | + | ⬛ | / | |
| | + | | + | | **13** |
| **3** | | **11** | | **3** | |

60

# SQUARE SUM

## #9

| | | | | | |
|---|---|---|---|---|---|
| | − | | + | | 4 |
| + | ■ | − | ■ | + | |
| | − | | X | | 35 |
| X | ■ | X | ■ | + | |
| | + | | + | | 11 |
| 68 | | 5 | | 2 | |

## #11

| | | | | | |
|---|---|---|---|---|---|
| | + | | − | | 9 |
| + | ■ | + | ■ | + | |
| | + | | X | | 9 |
| X | ■ | − | ■ | + | |
| | + | | X | | 91 |
| 28 | | 1 | | 15 | |

## #10

| | | | | | |
|---|---|---|---|---|---|
| | + | | X | | 63 |
| + | ■ | + | ■ | + | |
| | − | | X | | 25 |
| − | ■ | X | ■ | / | |
| | + | | X | | 42 |
| 5 | | 18 | | 2 | |

## #12

| | | | | | |
|---|---|---|---|---|---|
| | + | | + | | 17 |
| + | ■ | + | ■ | + | |
| | − | | X | | 16 |
| X | ■ | X | ■ | + | |
| | + | | / | | 4 |
| 15 | | 63 | | 13 | |

# WORD TRAIN

# WORD TRAIN

## INSTRUCTIONS TO PLAY

WORD TRAIN IS A FUN BUT CHALLENGING PUZZLE THAT IS SURE TO KEEP YOUR BRAIN HEALTHY. GO GRAB A PENCIL OR PEN AND GET STARTED!!

1. START FROM THE HIGHLIGHTED CELL AND MOVE UP OR DOWN OR RIGHT OR LEFT TO KEEP ADDING LETTERS TO FORM MEANINGFUL WORDS RELEVANT TO THE PROVIDED THEME. YOU CAN ONLY MOVE VERTICALLY OR HORIZONTALLY.
2. AFTER COMPLETING A WORD, MOVE ON TO FIND THE NEXT WORD SIMILARLY - THE FIRST LETTER OF THE SECOND WORD STARTS FROM AN UNUSED LETTER EITHER UP OR DOWN OR LEFT OR RIGHT TO THE LAST LETTER OF THE FIRST WORD.
3. THE TRAIN SHOULD EXTEND TO INCLUDE ALL THE 81 LETTERS IN THE GRID

THEME: PARK

WORDS:
PICNIC, TREES, SWINGS, SLIDES, BENCH, POND, PLAY AREA, DUCK, FOUNTAIN, TRAILS, BARBECUE, NATURE, SQUIRRELS

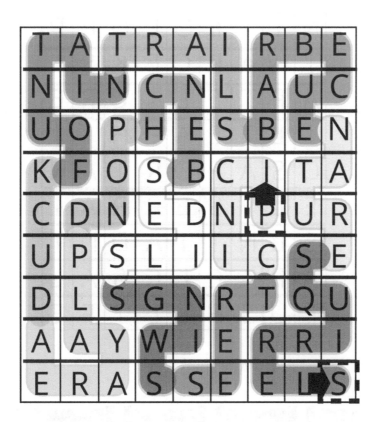

## WORD TRAIN #1

| D | A | L | F | G | Z | S | O | P |
|---|---|---|---|---|---|---|---|---|
| O | S | H | I | N | O | N | R | T |
| P | H | S | M | A | O | E | A | R |
| I | U | T | F | R | M | L | I | T |
| R | E | T | G | N | E | A | A | L |
| T | R | S | T | I | D | R | N | D |
| S | E | P | H | G | I | E | C | S |
| U | E | D | L | I | T | M | A | P |
| C | O | F | G | N | I | A | C | E |

PHOTOGRAPHY

## WORD TRAIN #2

| N | T | T | E | O | L | O | R | P |
|---|---|---|---|---|---|---|---|---|
| I | W | A | R | C | E | K | S | L |
| A | P | T | E | L | T | C | R | E |
| I | L | T | E | A | P | H | I | I |
| O | S | A | P | O | R | T | A | N |
| E | L | V | S | E | P | R | A | I |
| S | B | N | T | I | A | D | N | T |
| A | R | A | C | L | C | S | A | L |
| E | U | S | H | L | L | I | F | E |

PAINTING

## WORD TRAIN #3

| R | U | R | E | R | O | T | S | D |
|---|---|---|---|---|---|---|---|---|
| N | T | E | I | F | T | C | A | R |
| S | S | E | G | E | R | C | S | N |
| H | A | D | R | D | O | U | P | O |
| C | R | C | A | I | C | S | C | Y |
| P | U | L | C | T | A | L | A | E |
| E | A | E | T | D | E | H | S | L |
| C | R | U | N | I | D | I | T | L |
| N | A | O | C | S | R | E | R | O |

SHOPPING

## WORD TRAIN #4

| H | A | T | I | E | R | N | E | R |
|---|---|---|---|---|---|---|---|---|
| D | L | F | M | N | R | O | T | E |
| L | E | Y | E | O | W | C | D | D |
| F | I | E | L | L | C | D | E | N |
| D | I | M | E | E | A | R | F | E |
| R | E | F | E | R | F | I | F | R |
| E | T | U | T | I | A | G | P | E |
| S | U | B | S | T | S | O | E | E |
| M | U | I | D | A | T | A | L | K |

SOCCER

## WORD TRAIN #5

| | | | | | | | |
|---|---|---|---|---|---|---|---|
| L | E | S | S | I | N | G | S | H |
| B | L | I | M | M | E | O | H | A |
| R | Y | F | A | B | V | L | N | R |
| E | P | E | D | E | O | I | I | V |
| H | A | T | U | R | N | D | K | E |
| T | R | I | R | G | Y | A | P | S |
| A | A | T | A | T | P | U | M | T |
| G | D | U | R | S | A | E | A | F |
| S | E | T | K | E | Y | F | L | L |

THANKS GIVING

## WORD TRAIN #6

| | | | | | | | |
|---|---|---|---|---|---|---|---|
| S | D | F | P | F | P | S | S | B |
| A | N | L | I | L | O | E | L | O |
| S | L | L | E | H | S | A | L | A |
| T | I | D | E | E | C | K | U | R |
| I | B | E | R | N | O | S | G | D |
| K | E | S | C | H | M | E | A | W |
| I | V | S | S | A | M | K | L | A |
| N | A | U | N | N | N | D | U | N |
| I | W | G | N | I | A | T | S | E |

BEACH

# LITTLE WORDS

# LITTLE WORDS

CREATE AS MANY POSSIBLE LITTLE WORDS OF ANY LENGTH FROM THE WORDS BELOW !

JOURNEY

DELIGHT

BLUEPRINT

DAUGHTER

# LITTLE WORDS

CREATE AS MANY POSSIBLE LITTLE WORDS OF ANY LENGTH FROM THE WORDS BELOW !

BLUNDER

ABSOLVE

SECURITY

HOSPITAL

# LITTLE WORDS

CREATE AS MANY POSSIBLE LITTLE WORDS OF ANY LENGTH FROM THE WORDS BELOW !

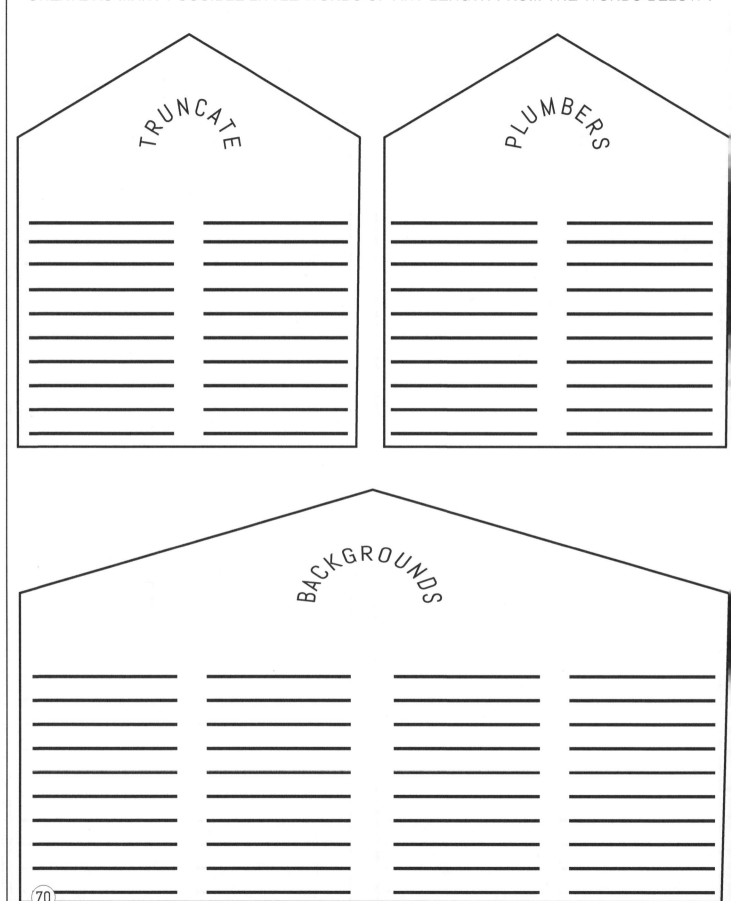

TRUNCATE

PLUMBERS

BACKGROUNDS

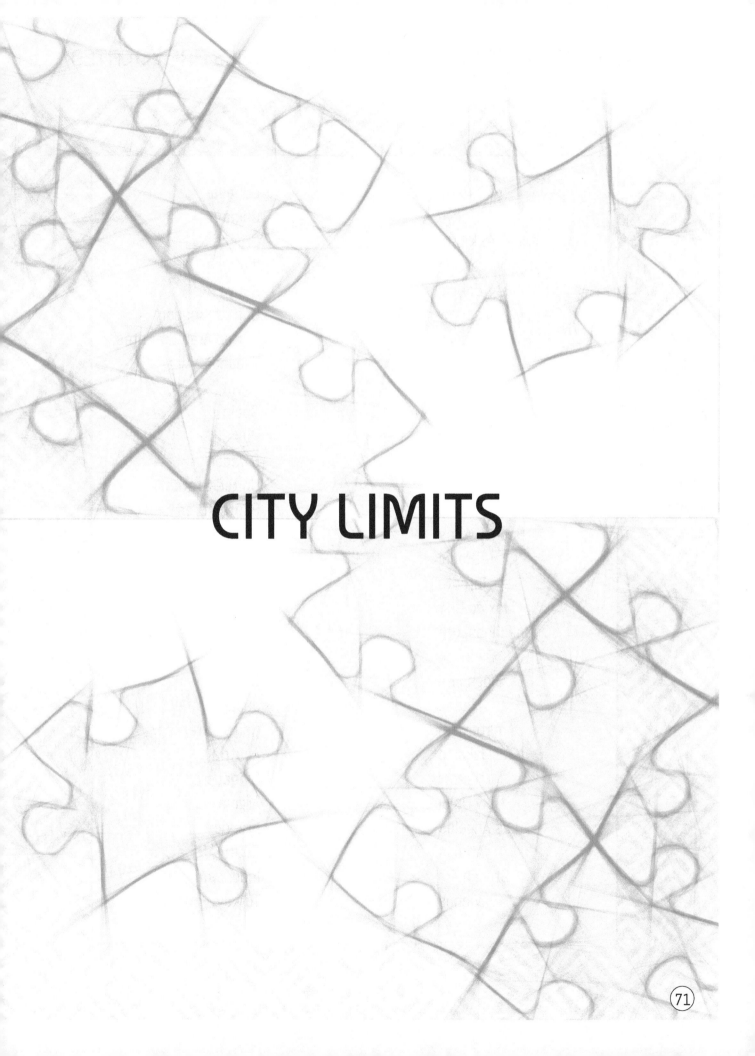

# CITY LIMITS

# IDENTIFY THE COUNTRIES WHERE THE CITIES ARE LOCATED

| | |
|---|---|
| Paris | Canada |
| Tokyo | China |
| New York City | Greece |
| London | India |
| Beijing | Kenya |
| Moscow | United Kingdom |
| Sydney | United Arab Emirates |
| Rome | Thailand |
| Cairo | Egypt |
| Rio de Janeiro | Spain |
| Istanbul | Russia |
| Mumbai | Sweden |
| Berlin | United States |
| Dubai | South Korea |
| Buenos Aires | Australia |
| Seoul | Mexico |
| Toronto | India |
| Mexico City | Brazil |
| Johannesburg | Netherlands |
| Bangkok | Italy |
| Singapore | Germany |
| Madrid | Japan |
| Amsterdam | United States |
| Jakarta | Austria |
| Nairobi | Singapore |
| New Delhi | Argentina |
| Los Angeles | France |
| Athens | South Africa |
| Stockholm | Indonesia |
| Vienna | Turkey |

# IDENTIFY THE U.S. STATES WHERE THE CITIES ARE LOCATED

Jersey City     _ _ _ _ _ _ _ _ _ _ _

Albany     _ _ _ _ _ _ _ _ _

Chicago     _ _ _ _ _ _ _ _

Houston     _ _ _ _ _

Phoenix     _ _ _ _ _ _ _

Philadelphia     _ _ _ _ _ _ _ _ _ _ _ _

San Antonio     _ _ _ _ _

San Diego     _ _ _ _ _ _ _ _ _ _

New Haven     _ _ _ _ _ _ _ _ _ _ _

Providence     _ _ _ _ _ _ _ _ _ _ _ _

Atlanta     _ _ _ _ _ _ _

Jacksonville     _ _ _ _ _ _ _

San Francisco     _ _ _ _ _ _ _ _ _ _

Indianapolis     _ _ _ _ _ _ _

Columbus     _ _ _ _

Fort Worth     _ _ _ _ _

Charlotte     _ _ _ _ _ _ _ _ _ _ _ _ _ _

Seattle     _ _ _ _ _ _ _ _ _ _

Denver     _ _ _ _ _ _ _ _

Washington     _ _ .

Boston     _ _ _ _ _ _ _ _ _ _ _ _ _ _ _

El Paso     _ _ _ _ _

Nashville     _ _ _ _ _ _ _ _ _

Detroit     _ _ _ _ _ _ _ _

Portland     _ _ _ _ _ _

Memphis     _ _ _ _ _ _ _ _ _

Oklahoma City     _ _ _ _ _ _ _ _

Las Vegas     _ _ _ _ _ _

Baltimore     _ _ _ _ _ _ _ _

Louisville     _ _ _ _ _ _ _ _

# TRIVIA LADDER

# TRIVIA LADDER

**#1**

- FIRST VOWEL
- CHEMICAL SYMBOL FOR GOLD
- OPPOSITE OF COLD
- ABBREVIATION FOR PROFESSOR
- THE BLUE PLANET
- WHEN MIXED WITH BLUE MAKES GREEN
- LARGEST OCEAN ON EARTH
- CAPITAL CITY OF AUSTRALIA
- FIVE-POINTED STAR
- WORDS THAT READ THE SAME WHEN READ BACKWARD

WRITE DOWN THE SHADED LETTERS _____

SOLVE THE ANAGRAM TO FIND THE NAME OF AN AMERICAN PRESIDENT [_____]

**#2**

- LAST ALPHABET
- ABBREVIATION OF CALIFORNIA
- DIAGRAMMATIC REPRESENTATION OF A GEOGRAPHY
- LARGEST CONTINENT
- MUSICAL INSTRUMENT PLAYED USING A KEYBOARD
- RINGED PLANET
- BIRD WITH BEAUTIFUL TAIL FEATHERS
- THE GALAXY WE LIVE IN
- THIS RETURNS TO THE THROWER WHEN THROWN
- WHAT AMAZON IS

SHADED LETTERS _____

A HOLLYWOOD STAR [_____]

# TRIVIA LADDER

**#3**

First consonant

Refers to the years after birth of Jesus

The star around which the earth orbits.

Planet known as the "Red Planet"

A sweet, viscous food substance made by bees

One of the world's largest desert

Six-sided polygon

Five-sided polygon

Decrease in price in economy

Group of drugs used to reduce sensation during surgery

SHADED LETTERS _____

A GREAT SPRINTER

**#4**

First person singular pronoun

Abbreviation for the state of Texas

This is mightier than the sword

Bird known for its distinctive "caw-caw" sound

The largest mammal in the world, which lives in the ocean.

Bird known for its ability to mimic human speech

World's highest mountain

Grassy plain with few trees

MIB actor

A person who practices astrology

SHADED LETTERS _____

YOU BOUNCE ON THESE FOR FUN

# ANSWERS

# STANDING TALL #1

1. THE NUMBER IS DIVISIBLE BY 3 - 147, 12, 999, 225, 354, 795, 168, 333, 207, 462, 903, 105, 297, 372, 429, 123, 180, 303, 771, 30
2. THE NUMBER IS DIVISIBLE BY 7 - 2345, 161, 168, 154, 910, 462, 903, 105, 175, 707, 133, 308, 805, 728, 28
3. THE NUMBER ENDS WITH A 0 - 500, 220, 550, 910, 1010, 180, 30, 320
4. THE NUMBER ENDS WITH A 5 - 2345, 895, 225, 795, 105, 175, 55, 805
5. THE NUMBER IS DIVISIBLE BY 11 - 22, 319, 1111, 88, 473
6. ALL POSSIBLE NUMBER OF DAYS IN A MONTH - 28, 29, 30, 31
7. THE NUMBER IS DIVISIBLE BY 8 - 808, 88, 824, 1648

ANSWER: 769

# STANDING TALL #2

1. NUMBER OF LETTERS IN WEEKDAYS - 6(SUNDAY, MONDAY, FRIDAY),7(TUESDAY),8(THURSDAY, SATURDAY),9(WEDNESDAY)
2. NUMBER OF LETTERS IN MONTHS - 3(MAY), 4(JUNE, JULY), 5(MARCH, APRIL), 6(AUGUST), 7(JANUARY, OCTOBER), 8(FEBRUARY, NOVEMBER, DECEMBER), 9(SEPTEMBER)
3. A DOZEN - 12
4. POSSIBLE NUMBER OF DAYS IN A MONTH - 28, 29, 30, 31
5. POSSIBLE NUMBER OF DAYS IN A YEAR - 365, 366
6. JUNETEENTH IS CELEBRATED ON THIS DAY OF JUNE - 19
7. THE INKTOBER MONTH IN NUMERALS - 10
8. AN UNLUCKY NUMBER - 13
9. 2 MINIMUM AGES FOR DRIVING LICENSE - 16, 18
10. IF GEORGE WASHINGTON IS 1, WHAT IS JOE BIDEN? - 46
11. THIS APOLLO LANDED THE FIRST MEN IN SPACE - 11
12. NUMBER OF US STATES - 50
13. IF AN INTERNET USER FOLLOWS A BROKEN OR DEAD LINK, THEY WILL TYPICALLY FIND AN ERROR PAGE WITH WHICH NUMBER ERROR MESSAGE - 404
14. US EMERGENCY CONTACT NUMBER - 911
15. WHICH AGE DO YOU HAVE TO REACH TO BE ELIGIBLE TO BECOME PRESIDENT OF THE UNITED STATES - 35
16. SEXAGENARIAN IS ABOVE THIS AGE - 60
17. SEPTUAGENARIAN IS ABOVE THIS AGE - 70
18. HOW MANY NUMBERS FROM 1 TO 99 DO NOT HAVE A,B,C,D? - 99
19. HOW MANY MILLIONS MAKE A BILLION? - 1000
20. IF APPLE IS 5 AND BANANA IS 6, WHAT IS UNCOPYRIGHTABLE? - 15
21. 4! - 24
22. SUICIDE PREVENTION NUMBER - 511
23. AT WHAT FAHRENHEIT DOES WATER FREEZE? - 32
24. THE YEAR OF US INDEPENDENCE - 1776
25. NUMBER OF YEARS THAT MAKE A SILVER JUBILEE - 25
26. NUMBER OF YEARS THAT MAKE A GOLDEN JUBILEE - 50
27. TWITTER'S NEW NAME IS ROMAN NUMERIC FORM OF THIS NUMBER - 10
28. HIGHEST PRIME NUMBER LESSER THAN 55 - 53
29. PRIME NUMBERS BETWEEN 40 AND 50 - 41, 43, 47
30. 2 CUBED + 2 SQUARED + 2! - 14
31. ONE QUARTER OF ONE THIRD OF 24 - 2
32. HOW MANY OZ MAKES A GALLON? - 128
33. SUM OF FIRST 6 NUMBERS OF A FIBONACCI SERIES - 1+1+2+3+5+8=20
34. YEAR WHEN PULP FICTION, THE SHAWSHANK REDEMPTION, AND JURASSIC PARK RELEASED - 1994
35. SUMMER OF '_ _? - 69
36. ONE ANGLE IN A RIGHT TRIANGLE IS 49, WHAT IS THE OTHER ANGLE? 51

ANSWER: 22

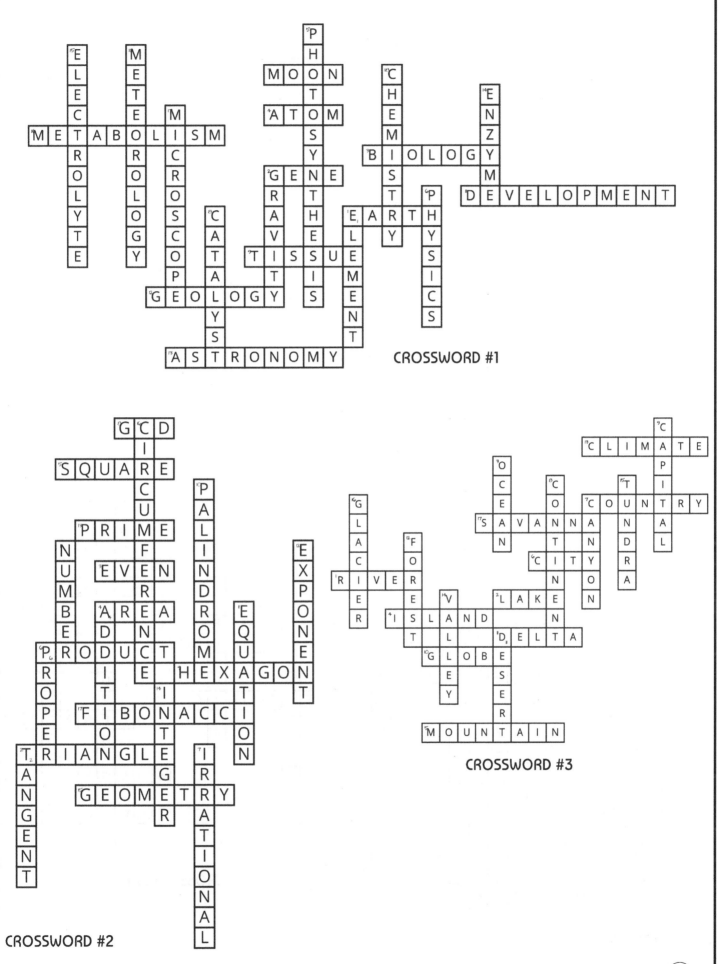

CROSSWORD #1

CROSSWORD #2

CROSSWORD #3

CROSSWORD #5

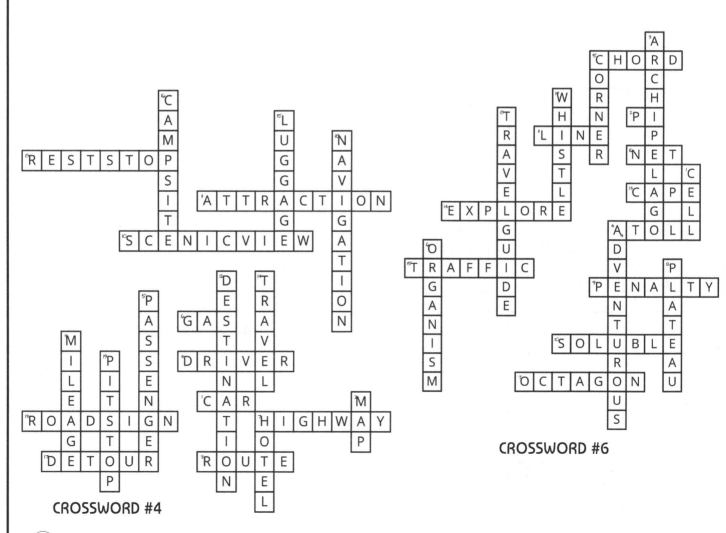

CROSSWORD #4

CROSSWORD #6

# KAKURO #1

| ■ | 11↓ | 36↓ | 7↓ | 41↓ | 24↓ | 12↓ | 9↓ | 19↓ |
|---|---|---|---|---|---|---|---|---|
| 39→ | 1 | 9 | 7 | 8 | 5 | 3 | 4 | 2 |
| 8→ | 6 | 2 | 29→/18↓ | 3 | 9 | 8 | 5 | 4 |
| 28→ | 4 | 5 | 6 | 9 | 3 | 1 | 8→/27↓ | 8 |
| ■ | 22→/14↓ | 4 | 5 | 7 | 6 | 6→/4↓ | 1 | 5 |
| 28→ | 5 | 7 | 3 | 2 | 1 | 4 | 6 | 11↓ |
| 18→ | 8 | 1 | 4 | 5 | 5↓ | 13→/8↓ | 7 | 6 |
| 9→ | 1 | 8 | 25→/6↓ | 6 | 2 | 3 | 9 | 5 |
| ■ | 19→ | 6 | 1 | 3 | 5 | 4 | ■ | ■ |

# KAKURO #2

| ■ | 36↓ | 43↓ | 19↓ | 37↓ | ■ | 11↓ | 23↓ | 3↓ |
|---|---|---|---|---|---|---|---|---|
| 14→ | 1 | 3 | 4 | 6 | 16→/14↓ | 4 | 9 | 3 |
| 35→ | 2 | 4 | 6 | 5 | 3 | 7 | 8 | 29↓ |
| 29→ | 7 | 5 | 9 | 2 | 6 | 7→/14↓ | 6 | 1 |
| 13→ | 5 | 8 | 12→/14↓ | 9 | 1 | 2 | 8→ | 8 |
| 32→ | 8 | 1 | 9 | 3 | 4 | 7 | 4→/13↓ | 4 |
| 19→ | 6 | 7 | 5 | 1 | 18→/14↓ | 5 | 6 | 7 |
| 9→ | 3 | 6 | 12→ | 4 | 8 | 12→/1↓ | 3 | 9 |
| 13→ | 4 | 9 | 18→ | 7 | 6 | 1 | 4 | ■ |

# KAKURO #3

| ■ | 19↓ | 38↓ | ■ | 2↓ | 19↓ | ■ | 4↓ | ■ | 4↓ | 2↓ |
|---|---|---|---|---|---|---|---|---|---|---|
| 13→ | 4 | 9 | 5→ | 2 | 3 | 4→/5↓ | 4 | 5→/3↓ | 3 | 2 |
| 5→ | 2 | 3 | 27↓ | 7→/13↓ | 5 | 2 | 4→/8↓ | 3 | 1 | ■ |
| 37→ | 9 | 6 | 2 | 5 | 4 | 3 | 8 | 19↓ | 29↓ | 14↓ |
| 26→ | 1 | 8 | 4 | 6 | 7 | ■ | 15→/28↓ | 2 | 9 | 4 |
| 13→ | 3 | 7 | 1 | 2 | 4↓ | 19→/22↓ | 4 | 8 | 5 | 2 |
| ■ | 14→/16↓ | 5 | 9 | 30→/11↓ | 4 | 6 | 2 | 9 | 8 | 1 |
| 1→ | 1 | 14→/21↓ | 8 | 6 | 8→/15↓ | 1 | 7 | 13→ | 6 | 7 |
| 40→ | 9 | 8 | 3 | 5 | 7 | 2 | 6 | 1→/6↓ | 1 | 10↓ |
| 10→ | 4 | 6 | 1↓ | 14→/3↓ | 3 | 4 | 1 | 6 | 1→/5↓ | 1 |
| 35→ | 2 | 7 | 1 | 3 | 5 | 9 | 8 | 14→ | 5 | 9 |

# KAKURO #4

| ■ | 9↓ | 13↓ | 10↓ | 36↓ | ■ | 12↓ | ■ | 6↓ |
|---|---|---|---|---|---|---|---|---|
| 18→ | 8 | 7 | 2 | 1 | 4→/16↓ | 4 | 6→/13↓ | 6 |
| 34→ | 1 | 4 | 8 | 2 | 3 | 7 | 9 | 9↓ |
| ■ | 2→/23↓ | 2 | 25→/8↓ | 7 | 8 | 1 | 4 | 5 |
| 8→ | 8 | 13→/24↓ | 2 | 6 | 5 | 11↓ | 4→/26↓ | 4 |
| 23→ | 9 | 5 | 6 | 3 | 10→/10↓ | 2 | 8 | 5↓ |
| 10→ | 2 | 8 | 32→/6↓ | 4 | 8 | 9 | 6 | 5 |
| 25→ | 1 | 9 | 5 | 8 | 2 | 9→/2↓ | 9 | 9↓ |
| 11→ | 3 | 2 | 1 | 5 | 14→ | 2 | 3 | 9 |

## KAKURO #5

| ■ | 21↓ | 15↓ | 8↓ | 26↓ | 21↓ | 36↓ | ■ | ■ |
|---|---|---|---|---|---|---|---|---|
| 27→ | 9 | 6 | 2 | 4 | 5 | 1 | ■ | 25↓ |
| 30→ | 5 | 8 | 6 | 1 | 7 | 3 | 8→ 8↓ | 8 |
| 8→ | 7 | 1 | 29→ 18↓ | 8 | 9 | 4 | 1 | 7 |
| ■ | 17↓ | 9→ | 3 | 6 | 10→ 14↓ | 2 | 7 | 1 |
| 3→ | 3 | 22→ 14↓ | 4 | 7 | 6 | 5 | 9→ 19↓ | 9 |
| 13→ | 6 | 5 | 2 | 12→ 9↓ | 2 | 6 | 4 | ■ |
| 38→ | 7 | 2 | 9 | 5 | 1 | 8 | 6 | 3↓ |
| 8→ | 1 | 7 | 28→ | 4 | 5 | 7 | 9 | 3 |

## KAKURO #6

| ■ | ■ | 5↓ | 41↓ | ■ | 13↓ | ■ | 16↓ | 18↓ |
|---|---|---|---|---|---|---|---|---|
| ■ | 8→ 32↓ | 3 | 5 | 5→ 34↓ | 5 | 9→ 1↓ | 1 | 8 |
| 40→ | 4 | 2 | 7 | 3 | 8 | 1 | 9 | 6 |
| 5→ | 5 | 17→ 11↓ | 8 | 9 | 11↓ | 10→ 26↓ | 6 | 4 |
| 30→ | 6 | 5 | 1 | 2 | 7 | 9 | 5↓ | 18↓ |
| 37→ | 9 | 6 | 3 | 7 | 4 | 2 | 5 | 1 |
| 8→ | 8 | 17→ 2↓ | 9 | 8 | 8→ 3↓ | 8 | 7→ 8↓ | 7 |
| ■ | 29→ 5↓ | 2 | 6 | 4 | 3 | 1 | 5 | 8 |
| 5→ | 5 | 3→ | 2 | 1 | 11→ | 6 | 3 | 2 |

## KAKURO #7

| ■ | 32↓ | 6↓ | ■ | 17↓ | 43↓ | 26↓ | 21↓ | 29↓ |
|---|---|---|---|---|---|---|---|---|
| 7→ | 1 | 6 | 27→ 9↓ | 2 | 6 | 8 | 4 | 7 |
| 6→ | 6 | 35→ 13↓ | 9 | 3 | 5 | 4 | 8 | 6 |
| 9→ | 3 | 6 | 22→ 2↓ | 8 | 3 | 1 | 6 | 4 |
| 37→ | 5 | 7 | 2 | 4 | 1 | 6 | 3 | 9 |
| 9→ | 9 | 1 | 14↓ | 11→ | 9 | 2 | 3→ 12↓ | 3 |
| 16→ | 8 | 1 | 7 | 16→ 16↓ | 4 | 5 | 7 | 9 |
| ■ | 5↓ | 19→ 8↓ | 4 | 7 | 8 | 11→ | 2 | 9 |
| 32→ | 5 | 8 | 3 | 9 | 7 | 3→ | 3 | ■ |

## KAKURO #8

| ■ | 2↓ | 15↓ | 1↓ | 20↓ | 12↓ | 28↓ | 38↓ | 10↓ | ■ | 27↓ |
|---|---|---|---|---|---|---|---|---|---|---|
| 38→ | 2 | 9 | 1 | 6 | 3 | 8 | 5 | 4 | 2→ | 2 |
| ■ | 6→ 1↓ | 6 | 21→ | 9 | 1 | 3 | 2 | 6 | 9→ 42↓ | |
| 1→ | 1 | 16↓ | 21→ 7↓ | 2 | 8 | 4 | 7 | 12→ 10↓ | 5 | 7 |
| ■ | 6→ | 1 | 2 | 3 | 22→ 31↓ | 6 | 4 | 8 | | |
| 5→ 29↓ | 4 | 1 | 35→ 21↓ | 4 | 7 | 9 | 2 | 8 | 5 | |
| 28→ | 9 | 5 | 4 | 7 | 3 | 3→ 4↓ | 3 | 10→ 10↓ | 9 | 1 |
| 14→ | 8 | 6 | 30→ 19↓ | 9 | 2 | 4 | 8 | 1 | 6 | 12↓ |
| 3→ | 3 | 20→ 8↓ | 7 | 5 | 8 | 11↓ | 11→ | 4 | 2 | 5 |
| 18→ | 7 | 3 | 8 | 8→ 6↓ | 5 | 3 | 12→ 7↓ | 5 | 4 | 3 |
| 41→ | 2 | 5 | 4 | 6 | 9 | 8 | 7 | 11→ | 7 | 4 |

# CRYPTOGRAM

CRYPTOGRAM #1
1. THE ONLY THING WE HAVE TO FEAR IS FEAR ITSELF.
2. LET US SACRIFICE OUR TODAY SO THAT OUR CHILDREN CAN HAVE A BETTER TOMORROW.
3. ASK NOT WHAT YOUR COUNTRY CAN DO FOR YOU; ASK WHAT YOU CAN DO FOR YOUR COUNTRY.
4. I HAVE A DREAM.
5. TEAR DOWN THIS WALL!
6. THE ONLY REAL PRISON IS FEAR, AND THE ONLY REAL FREEDOM IS FREEDOM FROM FEAR.
7. THE TIME FOR THE HEALING OF THE WOUNDS HAS COME.
8. IN THE END, IT'S NOT THE YEARS IN YOUR LIFE THAT COUNT. IT'S THE LIFE IN YOUR YEARS.

CRYPTOGRAM #2
1. LET US WORK TOGETHER TO BUILD A CULTURE THAT CHERISHES INNOCENT LIFE.
2. GIVE ME LIBERTY, OR GIVE ME DEATH!
3. I AM THE CAPTAIN OF MY SOUL.
4. BLOOD ALONE MOVES THE WHEELS OF HISTORY.
5. THE ONLY GUIDE TO A MAN IS HIS CONSCIENCE.
6. YOU CAN IMPRISON A MAN, BUT NOT AN IDEA. YOU CAN EXILE A MAN, BUT NOT AN IDEA.
7. CHANGE IS NEVER EASY, BUT ALWAYS POSSIBLE.
8. I BELIEVE THAT UNARMED TRUTH AND UNCONDITIONAL LOVE WILL HAVE THE FINAL WORD IN REALITY.

CRYPTOGRAM #3
1. THE BEST WAY TO PREDICT YOUR FUTURE IS TO CREATE IT.
2. LET US RESOLVE TO BE MASTERS, NOT THE VICTIMS, OF OUR HISTORY.
3. WE MUST LEARN TO LIVE TOGETHER AS BROTHERS OR PERISH TOGETHER AS FOOLS.
4. THE FUTURE DOESN'T BELONG TO THE FAINTHEARTED; IT BELONGS TO THE BRAVE.
5. WE MAKE A LIVING BY WHAT WE GET, BUT WE MAKE A LIFE BY WHAT WE GIVE.
6. THE GREATEST GLORY IN LIVING LIES NOT IN NEVER FALLING, BUT IN RISING EVERY TIME WE FALL.
7. THE WEAK CAN NEVER FORGIVE. FORGIVENESS IS THE ATTRIBUTE OF THE STRONG.
8. THE TIME IS ALWAYS RIGHT TO DO WHAT IS RIGHT.

CRYPTOGRAM #4
1. WE CANNOT SOLVE OUR PROBLEMS WITH THE SAME THINKING WE USED WHEN WE CREATED THEM.
2. THE TRUE SIGN OF INTELLIGENCE IS NOT KNOWLEDGE BUT IMAGINATION.
3. A PERSON WHO NEVER MADE A MISTAKE NEVER TRIED ANYTHING NEW.
4. THE ONLY SOURCE OF KNOWLEDGE IS EXPERIENCE
5. EDUCATION IS WHAT REMAINS AFTER ONE HAS FORGOTTEN WHAT ONE HAS LEARNED IN SCHOOL
6. PURE MATHEMATICS IS, IN ITS WAY, THE POETRY OF LOGICAL IDEAS
7. LIFE IS LIKE RIDING A BICYCLE. TO KEEP YOUR BALANCE, YOU MUST KEEP MOVING
8. LOOK DEEP INTO NATURE, AND THEN YOU WILL UNDERSTAND EVERYTHING BETTER

CRYPTOGRAM #5
1. LIFE IS LIKE A BOX OF CHOCOLATES; YOU NEVER KNOW WHAT YOU'RE GONNA GET.
2. THERE'S NO PLACE LIKE HOME.
3. I'LL BE BACK.
4. KEEP YOUR FRIENDS CLOSE, BUT YOUR ENEMIES CLOSER.
5. YOU CAN'T HANDLE THE TRUTH!
6. MAY THE FORCE BE WITH YOU.
7. HOUSTON, WE HAVE A PROBLEM.
8. TO INFINITY AND BEYOND!

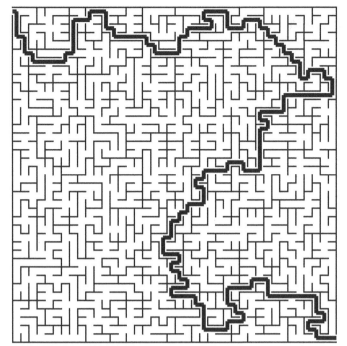

FIND YOUR WAY OUT #1

FIND YOUR WAY OUT #2

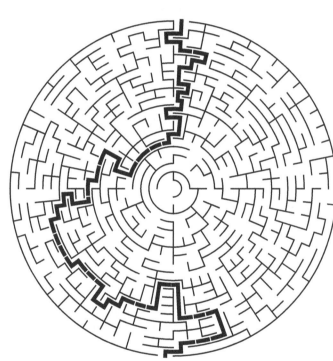

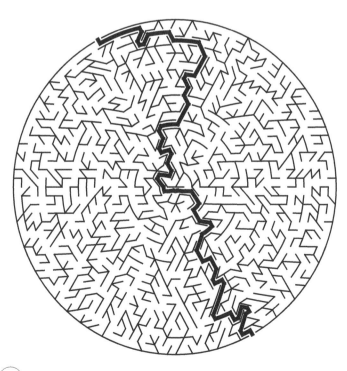

FIND YOUR WAY OUT #3

# FIND YOUR WAY OUT #4

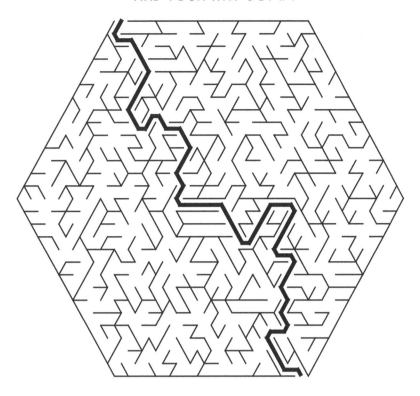

# FIND YOUR WAY OUT #5

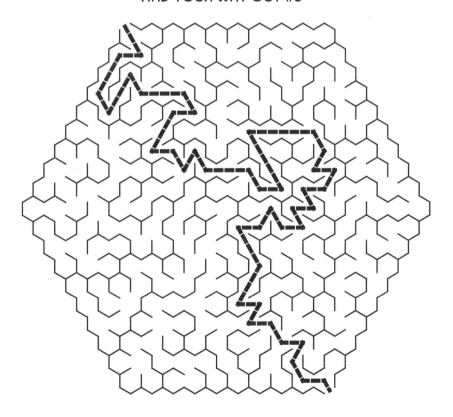

# WORD SEARCH #1

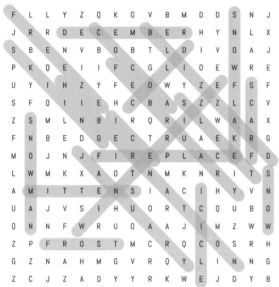
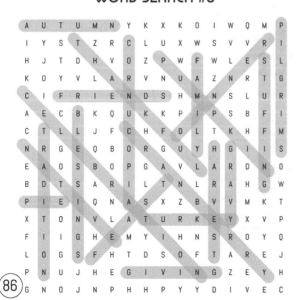

```
F W N I V Q A I P O P S I C L E
P L A T P J P H A M M O C K C R
K I I T L I S U N S C R E E N R
T Y N P E N C U N U S E C S M S
F H G T F R Q N Y G U Z R E G L
S I P G G L M L I R N S E A Y C
I U R B B A O E Z C S U A S T S
V C R E H A B P L Y H N M H D V
J A L F W X R T S O I G C E U P
F Z C E I O A B J Z L N L O L R A
O J W A M N R L E U E A C L Z R
O T D Z T O G K B C U S O S X A
S W I M M I N G S L U S N S P S
R I H G Y U O A M O Y E U E F O
M T E G B S A N D C A S T L E L
C X V V C Z Q I B E A C H S Y N
```

# WORD SEARCH #2

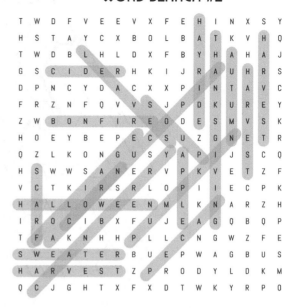

```
T W D F V E E V X F E H I N X S Y
H S T A Y C X B O L B A T K V H Q
T W D B L H L D X F B Y H A H A J
G S C I D E R H K I J R A U H R S
D P N C Y D A C X X P I N T A V C
F R Z N F Q V V S J P D K U R E Y
Z W B O N F I R E O D E S M V S K
H O E Y B E P E C S U Z G N E T Z
Q Z L K O N G U S Y A P I J S C Q
H S W W S A N E R V P K V E T Z F
V C T K I R S R L O P I I E C P K
H A L L O W E E N M L K N A R Z H
I R O C I B X F U J E A G Q B Q P
T F A K N H H P L L C N G W Z F E
S W E A T E R B U E P W A G B U S
H A R V E S T Z P R O D Y L D K M
Q C J G H T X F X D T W K Y R P O
```

# WORD SEARCH #3

```
F L L Y Z Q K G V B M D D S N J
J R R D E C E M B E R H Y N L X
S B E N V B O B T L D I V O A J
P K Q E I I F C G L I O E W R E
U Y I H Z Y F E O W Y Z E F S F
S F Q I I E H C B A S Z Z L C V
Z S M L N B I R Q R I L W A A X
F N B E D G E C T R U A E K R G
M O J N J F I R E P L A C E F D
L W M K X A O T N M K N R I T S
A M I T T E N S I A C I H Y V N
U A J V S I H U O R T C Q U B O
Q N N F W R U O A A J I M Z W J
Z P F R O S T M C R Q C O S R H
G Z N A H M G V R Q Y L I N G
Z C J Z A D Y Y R K W E J D Y B
```

# WORD SEARCH #4

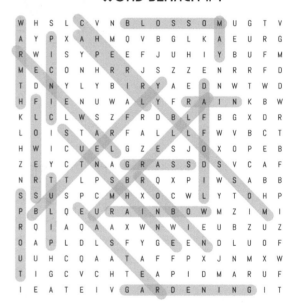

```
W H S L C V N B L O S S O M U G T V
A Y P X A H M Q V B G L K A E U R G
R W I S Y P E E F J U H I Y B U F M
M E C O N H R R J S Z Z E N R R F D
T D N Y L Y B I R Y A E D N W T W D
H F I E N U W A L Y F R A I N K B W
K L C L W S Z F R D B L F B G X D R
L O I S T A R F A L L L F W V B C T
H W I C U E L G Z E S J O X O P E B
Z E Y C T N A G R A S S D S V C A F
N R T T L P S B R Q X P I W S A B B
S S U S P C M H X O C W L Y T O H P
P B L Q E U R A I N B O W M Z I M I
R Q I A Q A A X W N W I E U B Z U Z
O A P L D L S F Y G E E N D L U O F
U U H C Q A A T A F F P X J N M X W
T I G C V C H T E A P I D M A R U F
I E A T E I V G A R D E N I N G I T
```

# WORD SEARCH #5

```
A U T U M N Y K X K O I W Q M P
I Y S T Z R C L U X W S V V R I
H J T D H V O Z P W F W L E S L
K O Y V L A R V N U A Z N R T G
C I F R I E N D S H M N S L U R
A E C B K Q U K K P I P S B F I
C T L L J F C F D L T K H F M K
N R G E Q B O R G U Y H G I I S
E A O S B O P G A V L A R D N O
B D T S A R I L T N L R A H G W
P I E I Q N A S X Z B V V M K T
X T O N V L A T U R K E Y E X V P
F I I G H E M Y I H N S R O Y Q
L O G S F H T D S O F T A R E J
P N U J H E G I V I N G E Z Y H
G N O J N P H H P Y Y D I V E C
```

# WORD SEARCH #6

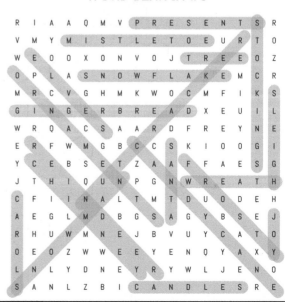

```
R I A A Q M V P R E S E N T S R
V M Y M I S T L E T O E U R T O
W E O O X O N V O J T R E E O Z
O P L A S N O W F L A K E M C R
M R C V G H M K W O C M F I K S
G I N G E R B R E A D X E U I L
W R Q A C S A A R D F R E Y N E
E R F W M G B C C S K I O O G I
Y C E B S E T Z A A F F A E S G
J T H I Q U N P G N W R E A T H
C F I I N A L T M T D U O D E H
A E G L M D B G S A G Y B S E J
R H U W M N E J B V U Y C A T O
O E O Z W W E E Y E N Q Y A X Y
L N L Y D N E Y R Y W L E N O G
S A N L Z B I C A N D L E S R E
```

# SUDOKU

## #1

| 9 | 8 | 6 | 2 | 4 | 5 | 3 | 7 | 1 |
|---|---|---|---|---|---|---|---|---|
| 1 | 4 | 7 | 6 | 9 | 3 | 8 | 2 | 5 |
| 3 | 2 | 5 | 1 | 8 | 7 | 9 | 6 | 4 |
| 8 | 5 | 1 | 3 | 6 | 4 | 7 | 9 | 2 |
| 7 | 6 | 3 | 5 | 2 | 9 | 1 | 4 | 8 |
| 4 | 9 | 2 | 7 | 1 | 8 | 5 | 3 | 6 |
| 5 | 3 | 8 | 4 | 7 | 2 | 6 | 1 | 9 |
| 2 | 1 | 9 | 8 | 3 | 6 | 4 | 5 | 7 |
| 6 | 7 | 4 | 9 | 5 | 1 | 2 | 8 | 3 |

## #2

| 6 | 8 | 9 | 2 | 7 | 1 | 5 | 4 | 3 |
|---|---|---|---|---|---|---|---|---|
| 5 | 2 | 1 | 8 | 4 | 3 | 7 | 6 | 9 |
| 7 | 4 | 3 | 5 | 6 | 9 | 2 | 1 | 8 |
| 4 | 9 | 8 | 7 | 5 | 6 | 3 | 2 | 1 |
| 2 | 3 | 7 | 4 | 1 | 8 | 9 | 5 | 6 |
| 1 | 5 | 6 | 9 | 3 | 2 | 8 | 7 | 4 |
| 3 | 7 | 5 | 1 | 8 | 4 | 6 | 9 | 2 |
| 8 | 1 | 2 | 6 | 9 | 7 | 4 | 3 | 5 |
| 9 | 6 | 4 | 3 | 2 | 5 | 1 | 8 | 7 |

## #3

| 2 | 9 | 5 | 1 | 4 | 6 | 3 | 7 | 8 |
|---|---|---|---|---|---|---|---|---|
| 6 | 1 | 8 | 9 | 7 | 3 | 4 | 2 | 5 |
| 7 | 3 | 4 | 8 | 2 | 5 | 9 | 1 | 6 |
| 8 | 6 | 3 | 4 | 1 | 9 | 2 | 5 | 7 |
| 5 | 2 | 9 | 7 | 6 | 8 | 1 | 4 | 3 |
| 4 | 7 | 1 | 3 | 5 | 2 | 8 | 6 | 9 |
| 1 | 8 | 2 | 6 | 9 | 7 | 5 | 3 | 4 |
| 9 | 5 | 7 | 2 | 3 | 4 | 6 | 8 | 1 |
| 3 | 4 | 6 | 5 | 8 | 1 | 7 | 9 | 2 |

## #4

| 5 | 6 | 3 | 4 | 7 | 2 | 1 | 9 | 8 |
|---|---|---|---|---|---|---|---|---|
| 8 | 1 | 9 | 3 | 6 | 5 | 2 | 4 | 7 |
| 2 | 7 | 4 | 1 | 8 | 9 | 3 | 5 | 6 |
| 9 | 5 | 7 | 8 | 2 | 3 | 6 | 1 | 4 |
| 1 | 8 | 6 | 9 | 5 | 4 | 7 | 2 | 3 |
| 3 | 4 | 2 | 6 | 1 | 7 | 9 | 8 | 5 |
| 6 | 9 | 5 | 7 | 4 | 1 | 8 | 3 | 2 |
| 4 | 3 | 8 | 2 | 9 | 6 | 5 | 7 | 1 |
| 7 | 2 | 1 | 5 | 3 | 8 | 4 | 6 | 9 |

SUDOKU

| 5 | 8 | 2 | 3 | 4 | 7 | 9 | 1 | 6 |
| 1 | 7 | 9 | 8 | 6 | 5 | 4 | 3 | 2 |
| 4 | 3 | 6 | 9 | 2 | 1 | 5 | 7 | 8 |
| 3 | 1 | 7 | 6 | 8 | 4 | 2 | 9 | 5 |
| 6 | 2 | 5 | 7 | 3 | 9 | 8 | 4 | 1 |
| 9 | 4 | 8 | 5 | 1 | 2 | 3 | 6 | 7 |
| 8 | 5 | 1 | 4 | 7 | 3 | 6 | 2 | 9 |
| 7 | 9 | 3 | 2 | 5 | 6 | 1 | 8 | 4 |
| 2 | 6 | 4 | 1 | 9 | 8 | 7 | 5 | 3 |

| 5 | 6 | 9 | 7 | 4 | 8 | 1 | 3 | 2 |
| 2 | 4 | 7 | 9 | 3 | 1 | 8 | 6 | 5 |
| 3 | 8 | 1 | 5 | 2 | 6 | 7 | 9 | 4 |
| 7 | 9 | 8 | 6 | 5 | 4 | 3 | 2 | 1 |
| 1 | 5 | 3 | 8 | 9 | 2 | 6 | 4 | 7 |
| 6 | 2 | 4 | 1 | 7 | 3 | 9 | 5 | 8 |
| 4 | 3 | 6 | 2 | 8 | 7 | 5 | 1 | 9 |
| 9 | 7 | 2 | 3 | 1 | 5 | 4 | 8 | 6 |
| 8 | 1 | 5 | 4 | 6 | 9 | 2 | 7 | 3 |

| 6 | 1 | 7 | 8 | 2 | 4 | 3 | 9 | 5 |
| 2 | 3 | 4 | 7 | 5 | 9 | 6 | 1 | 8 |
| 8 | 5 | 9 | 6 | 3 | 1 | 4 | 2 | 7 |
| 7 | 9 | 8 | 4 | 1 | 5 | 2 | 6 | 3 |
| 1 | 4 | 5 | 3 | 6 | 2 | 8 | 7 | 9 |
| 3 | 2 | 6 | 9 | 8 | 7 | 1 | 5 | 4 |
| 5 | 6 | 3 | 1 | 9 | 8 | 7 | 4 | 2 |
| 9 | 7 | 1 | 2 | 4 | 3 | 5 | 8 | 6 |
| 4 | 8 | 2 | 5 | 7 | 6 | 9 | 3 | 1 |

| 1 | 7 | 3 | 6 | 2 | 9 | 5 | 4 | 8 |
| 8 | 2 | 5 | 4 | 3 | 7 | 9 | 1 | 6 |
| 4 | 6 | 9 | 8 | 5 | 1 | 7 | 2 | 3 |
| 9 | 4 | 1 | 2 | 8 | 5 | 6 | 3 | 7 |
| 3 | 5 | 6 | 1 | 7 | 4 | 8 | 9 | 2 |
| 2 | 8 | 7 | 9 | 6 | 3 | 4 | 5 | 1 |
| 6 | 1 | 2 | 5 | 4 | 8 | 3 | 7 | 9 |
| 7 | 9 | 4 | 3 | 1 | 6 | 2 | 8 | 5 |
| 5 | 3 | 8 | 7 | 9 | 2 | 1 | 6 | 4 |

# SUDOKU

| 2 | 8 | 9 | 4 | 7 | 3 | 5 | 1 | 6 |
| 6 | 3 | 7 | 1 | 2 | 5 | 9 | 4 | 8 |
| 1 | 5 | 4 | 8 | 6 | 9 | 2 | 7 | 3 |
| 3 | 7 | 8 | 6 | 4 | 2 | 1 | 5 | 9 |
| 4 | 9 | 1 | 7 | 5 | 8 | 3 | 6 | 2 |
| 5 | 2 | 6 | 9 | 3 | 1 | 7 | 8 | 4 |
| 9 | 6 | 2 | 5 | 1 | 4 | 8 | 3 | 7 |
| 7 | 1 | 3 | 2 | 8 | 6 | 4 | 9 | 5 |
| 8 | 4 | 5 | 3 | 9 | 7 | 6 | 2 | 1 |

| 3 | 1 | 5 | 4 | 8 | 6 | 7 | 9 | 2 |
| 4 | 6 | 9 | 5 | 2 | 7 | 3 | 1 | 8 |
| 8 | 2 | 7 | 3 | 1 | 9 | 4 | 5 | 6 |
| 5 | 7 | 6 | 2 | 9 | 4 | 1 | 8 | 3 |
| 1 | 9 | 4 | 8 | 3 | 5 | 2 | 6 | 7 |
| 2 | 8 | 3 | 7 | 6 | 1 | 9 | 4 | 5 |
| 9 | 3 | 8 | 6 | 4 | 2 | 5 | 7 | 1 |
| 6 | 5 | 1 | 9 | 7 | 3 | 8 | 2 | 4 |
| 7 | 4 | 2 | 1 | 5 | 8 | 6 | 3 | 9 |

| 6 | 2 | 5 | 9 | 7 | 8 | 3 | 4 | 1 |
| 1 | 7 | 9 | 6 | 3 | 4 | 2 | 8 | 5 |
| 8 | 4 | 3 | 1 | 5 | 2 | 6 | 9 | 7 |
| 4 | 3 | 2 | 8 | 9 | 5 | 7 | 1 | 6 |
| 5 | 8 | 1 | 4 | 6 | 7 | 9 | 3 | 2 |
| 9 | 6 | 7 | 2 | 1 | 3 | 8 | 5 | 4 |
| 2 | 5 | 8 | 7 | 4 | 9 | 1 | 6 | 3 |
| 7 | 1 | 4 | 3 | 8 | 6 | 5 | 2 | 9 |
| 3 | 9 | 6 | 5 | 2 | 1 | 4 | 7 | 8 |

| 8 | 5 | 9 | 7 | 1 | 6 | 2 | 4 | 3 |
| 1 | 6 | 3 | 8 | 4 | 2 | 5 | 9 | 7 |
| 2 | 4 | 7 | 5 | 3 | 9 | 8 | 1 | 6 |
| 7 | 3 | 5 | 2 | 8 | 1 | 9 | 6 | 4 |
| 4 | 1 | 6 | 3 | 9 | 5 | 7 | 8 | 2 |
| 9 | 8 | 2 | 6 | 7 | 4 | 1 | 3 | 5 |
| 3 | 7 | 1 | 4 | 2 | 8 | 6 | 5 | 9 |
| 6 | 2 | 8 | 9 | 5 | 3 | 4 | 7 | 1 |
| 5 | 9 | 4 | 1 | 6 | 7 | 3 | 2 | 8 |

#13

| 1 | 16 | 11 | 14 | 7 | 10 | 6 | 15 | 13 | 5 | 4 | 8 | 12 | 2 | 3 | 9 |
|---|----|----|----|---|----|---|----|----|---|---|---|----|---|---|---|
| 6 | 15 | 13 | 4 | 14 | 16 | 9 | 5 | 1 | 12 | 3 | 2 | 7 | 10 | 11 | 8 |
| 2 | 3 | 5 | 7 | 13 | 12 | 11 | 8 | 10 | 15 | 16 | 9 | 6 | 14 | 4 | 1 |
| 8 | 10 | 9 | 12 | 1 | 2 | 3 | 4 | 6 | 7 | 11 | 14 | 16 | 5 | 15 | 13 |
| 10 | 7 | 1 | 6 | 5 | 3 | 2 | 9 | 16 | 13 | 15 | 12 | 11 | 8 | 14 | 4 |
| 16 | 8 | 3 | 13 | 11 | 1 | 10 | 12 | 4 | 6 | 14 | 7 | 15 | 9 | 2 | 5 |
| 11 | 4 | 12 | 9 | 16 | 15 | 7 | 14 | 3 | 2 | 8 | 5 | 10 | 13 | 1 | 6 |
| 15 | 14 | 2 | 5 | 6 | 4 | 8 | 13 | 9 | 11 | 1 | 10 | 3 | 7 | 16 | 12 |
| 3 | 2 | 15 | 11 | 9 | 5 | 14 | 1 | 7 | 8 | 13 | 6 | 4 | 12 | 10 | 16 |
| 14 | 9 | 10 | 16 | 12 | 8 | 4 | 6 | 15 | 1 | 2 | 11 | 13 | 3 | 5 | 7 |
| 7 | 12 | 6 | 8 | 2 | 13 | 16 | 3 | 14 | 10 | 5 | 4 | 1 | 11 | 9 | 15 |
| 13 | 5 | 4 | 1 | 10 | 11 | 15 | 7 | 12 | 3 | 9 | 16 | 14 | 6 | 8 | 2 |
| 5 | 13 | 14 | 2 | 4 | 7 | 12 | 11 | 8 | 16 | 10 | 15 | 9 | 1 | 6 | 3 |
| 4 | 1 | 8 | 10 | 3 | 6 | 5 | 16 | 11 | 9 | 12 | 13 | 2 | 15 | 7 | 14 |
| 9 | 11 | 7 | 3 | 15 | 14 | 13 | 2 | 5 | 4 | 6 | 1 | 8 | 16 | 12 | 10 |
| 12 | 6 | 16 | 15 | 8 | 9 | 1 | 10 | 2 | 14 | 7 | 3 | 5 | 4 | 13 | 11 |

# SUDOKU

14

| 2 | 6 | 5 | 3 | 9 | 4 | 1 | 7 | 8 |
|---|---|---|---|---|---|---|---|---|
| 8 | 3 | 9 | 7 | 1 | 6 | 4 | 5 | 2 |
| 1 | 4 | 7 | 2 | 5 | 8 | 9 | 3 | 6 |
| 6 | 1 | 3 | 9 | 2 | 5 | 8 | 4 | 7 |
| 7 | 9 | 2 | 4 | 8 | 1 | 3 | 6 | 5 |
| 4 | 5 | 8 | 6 | 7 | 3 | 2 | 9 | 1 |
| 5 | 2 | 6 | 1 | 3 | 9 | 7 | 8 | 4 |
| 3 | 8 | 1 | 5 | 4 | 7 | 6 | 2 | 9 |
| 9 | 7 | 4 | 8 | 6 | 2 | 5 | 1 | 3 |

#15

| 8 | 4 | 9 | 3 | 5 | 2 | 6 | 7 | 1 |
|---|---|---|---|---|---|---|---|---|
| 3 | 6 | 1 | 4 | 7 | 8 | 2 | 5 | 9 |
| 5 | 2 | 7 | 6 | 9 | 1 | 8 | 4 | 3 |
| 2 | 1 | 3 | 5 | 6 | 4 | 9 | 8 | 7 |
| 4 | 5 | 8 | 7 | 2 | 9 | 1 | 3 | 6 |
| 9 | 7 | 6 | 8 | 1 | 3 | 4 | 2 | 5 |
| 7 | 9 | 4 | 2 | 3 | 6 | 5 | 1 | 8 |
| 6 | 8 | 5 | 1 | 4 | 7 | 3 | 9 | 2 |
| 1 | 3 | 2 | 9 | 8 | 5 | 7 | 6 | 4 |

#16

| 2 | 3 | 7 | 4 | 9 | 5 | 8 | 1 | 6 |
|---|---|---|---|---|---|---|---|---|
| 8 | 5 | 6 | 2 | 1 | 7 | 4 | 9 | 3 |
| 4 | 9 | 1 | 8 | 6 | 3 | 5 | 2 | 7 |
| 1 | 7 | 4 | 5 | 8 | 2 | 6 | 3 | 9 |
| 5 | 8 | 2 | 6 | 3 | 9 | 1 | 7 | 4 |
| 9 | 6 | 3 | 7 | 4 | 1 | 2 | 5 | 8 |
| 6 | 2 | 5 | 9 | 7 | 8 | 3 | 4 | 1 |
| 7 | 1 | 8 | 3 | 5 | 4 | 9 | 6 | 2 |
| 3 | 4 | 9 | 1 | 2 | 6 | 7 | 8 | 5 |

#17

| 5 | 7 | 4 | 2 | 8 | 3 | 6 | 9 | 1 |
|---|---|---|---|---|---|---|---|---|
| 6 | 8 | 1 | 9 | 5 | 7 | 3 | 4 | 2 |
| 9 | 2 | 3 | 1 | 4 | 6 | 5 | 8 | 7 |
| 3 | 4 | 8 | 5 | 2 | 1 | 9 | 7 | 6 |
| 7 | 9 | 2 | 8 | 6 | 4 | 1 | 3 | 5 |
| 1 | 5 | 6 | 7 | 3 | 9 | 4 | 2 | 8 |
| 2 | 3 | 9 | 6 | 1 | 8 | 7 | 5 | 4 |
| 8 | 6 | 7 | 4 | 9 | 5 | 2 | 1 | 3 |
| 4 | 1 | 5 | 3 | 7 | 2 | 8 | 6 | 9 |

91

# SUDOKU

#18

| 8 | 5 | 7 | 1 | 16 | 14 | 2 | 11 | 12 | 15 | 9 | 4 | 3 | 6 | 13 | 10 |
|---|---|---|---|----|----|---|----|----|----|---|---|---|---|----|----|
| 10 | 12 | 13 | 16 | 6 | 4 | 8 | 7 | 3 | 1 | 11 | 2 | 14 | 5 | 15 | 9 |
| 11 | 9 | 14 | 15 | 10 | 13 | 5 | 3 | 6 | 16 | 7 | 8 | 1 | 2 | 12 | 4 |
| 6 | 3 | 2 | 4 | 12 | 15 | 9 | 1 | 14 | 5 | 10 | 13 | 11 | 16 | 8 | 7 |
| 16 | 15 | 10 | 13 | 5 | 12 | 3 | 4 | 9 | 11 | 14 | 7 | 8 | 1 | 2 | 6 |
| 14 | 8 | 9 | 7 | 11 | 2 | 6 | 13 | 4 | 12 | 5 | 1 | 15 | 10 | 16 | 3 |
| 5 | 2 | 11 | 6 | 7 | 8 | 1 | 9 | 16 | 10 | 15 | 3 | 4 | 13 | 14 | 12 |
| 1 | 4 | 3 | 12 | 15 | 16 | 10 | 14 | 2 | 13 | 8 | 6 | 5 | 9 | 7 | 11 |
| 2 | 10 | 1 | 3 | 14 | 6 | 12 | 8 | 11 | 7 | 4 | 16 | 9 | 15 | 5 | 13 |
| 13 | 11 | 16 | 5 | 3 | 10 | 15 | 2 | 1 | 9 | 6 | 12 | 7 | 8 | 4 | 14 |
| 12 | 7 | 4 | 9 | 13 | 1 | 11 | 5 | 8 | 14 | 2 | 15 | 10 | 3 | 6 | 16 |
| 15 | 14 | 6 | 8 | 9 | 7 | 4 | 16 | 5 | 3 | 13 | 10 | 2 | 12 | 11 | 1 |
| 7 | 13 | 12 | 2 | 8 | 9 | 14 | 10 | 15 | 6 | 1 | 11 | 16 | 4 | 3 | 5 |
| 9 | 16 | 5 | 10 | 4 | 3 | 13 | 15 | 7 | 2 | 12 | 14 | 6 | 11 | 1 | 8 |
| 3 | 1 | 8 | 11 | 2 | 5 | 7 | 6 | 13 | 4 | 16 | 9 | 12 | 14 | 10 | 15 |
| 4 | 6 | 15 | 14 | 1 | 11 | 16 | 12 | 10 | 8 | 3 | 5 | 13 | 7 | 9 | 2 |

# SUDOKU

## #19

| 7 | 9 | 6 | 3 | 4 | 1 | 5 | 8 | 2 |
|---|---|---|---|---|---|---|---|---|
| 3 | 1 | 4 | 8 | 5 | 2 | 6 | 9 | 7 |
| 2 | 5 | 8 | 9 | 7 | 6 | 3 | 4 | 1 |
| 6 | 2 | 9 | 1 | 8 | 3 | 7 | 5 | 4 |
| 1 | 7 | 3 | 5 | 9 | 4 | 8 | 2 | 6 |
| 8 | 4 | 5 | 2 | 6 | 7 | 9 | 1 | 3 |
| 4 | 8 | 1 | 6 | 3 | 5 | 2 | 7 | 9 |
| 9 | 3 | 2 | 7 | 1 | 8 | 4 | 6 | 5 |
| 5 | 6 | 7 | 4 | 2 | 9 | 1 | 3 | 8 |

## #20

| 5 | 9 | 1 | 3 | 6 | 8 | 7 | 4 | 2 |
|---|---|---|---|---|---|---|---|---|
| 4 | 2 | 7 | 1 | 9 | 5 | 8 | 6 | 3 |
| 3 | 8 | 6 | 4 | 7 | 2 | 5 | 9 | 1 |
| 2 | 7 | 4 | 8 | 5 | 9 | 3 | 1 | 6 |
| 6 | 3 | 9 | 2 | 1 | 7 | 4 | 5 | 8 |
| 8 | 1 | 5 | 6 | 4 | 3 | 2 | 7 | 9 |
| 7 | 5 | 3 | 9 | 2 | 1 | 6 | 8 | 4 |
| 9 | 6 | 8 | 7 | 3 | 4 | 1 | 2 | 5 |
| 1 | 4 | 2 | 5 | 8 | 6 | 9 | 3 | 7 |

## #21

| 4 | 2 | 6 | 8 | 9 | 7 | 3 | 1 | 5 |
|---|---|---|---|---|---|---|---|---|
| 3 | 8 | 7 | 6 | 1 | 5 | 2 | 9 | 4 |
| 9 | 5 | 1 | 3 | 4 | 2 | 8 | 6 | 7 |
| 8 | 7 | 2 | 4 | 3 | 9 | 6 | 5 | 1 |
| 1 | 9 | 3 | 5 | 6 | 8 | 7 | 4 | 2 |
| 6 | 4 | 5 | 2 | 7 | 1 | 9 | 8 | 3 |
| 2 | 1 | 9 | 7 | 8 | 4 | 5 | 3 | 6 |
| 5 | 3 | 4 | 9 | 2 | 6 | 1 | 7 | 8 |
| 7 | 6 | 8 | 1 | 5 | 3 | 4 | 2 | 9 |

## #22

| 2 | 5 | 4 | 8 | 6 | 7 | 9 | 1 | 3 |
|---|---|---|---|---|---|---|---|---|
| 7 | 8 | 9 | 5 | 3 | 1 | 6 | 4 | 2 |
| 1 | 6 | 3 | 9 | 2 | 4 | 5 | 7 | 8 |
| 6 | 1 | 2 | 4 | 9 | 3 | 8 | 5 | 7 |
| 8 | 4 | 5 | 2 | 7 | 6 | 1 | 3 | 9 |
| 9 | 3 | 7 | 1 | 8 | 5 | 4 | 2 | 6 |
| 3 | 7 | 1 | 6 | 4 | 9 | 2 | 8 | 5 |
| 4 | 2 | 6 | 7 | 5 | 8 | 3 | 9 | 1 |
| 5 | 9 | 8 | 3 | 1 | 2 | 7 | 6 | 4 |

# SUDOKU

## #23

| 7 | 8 | 2 | 3 | 9 | 1 | 4 | 5 | 6 |
| 4 | 1 | 6 | 8 | 2 | 5 | 3 | 7 | 9 |
| 5 | 3 | 9 | 4 | 7 | 6 | 2 | 8 | 1 |
| 3 | 2 | 4 | 7 | 1 | 8 | 9 | 6 | 5 |
| 1 | 9 | 7 | 6 | 5 | 3 | 8 | 2 | 4 |
| 8 | 6 | 5 | 9 | 4 | 2 | 7 | 1 | 3 |
| 6 | 4 | 3 | 5 | 8 | 7 | 1 | 9 | 2 |
| 9 | 7 | 1 | 2 | 6 | 4 | 5 | 3 | 8 |
| 2 | 5 | 8 | 1 | 3 | 9 | 6 | 4 | 7 |

## #24

| 7 | 4 | 5 | 1 | 3 | 2 | 6 | 8 | 9 |
| 6 | 2 | 1 | 5 | 8 | 9 | 3 | 7 | 4 |
| 8 | 3 | 9 | 4 | 6 | 7 | 2 | 5 | 1 |
| 2 | 1 | 8 | 7 | 5 | 4 | 9 | 3 | 6 |
| 4 | 9 | 6 | 3 | 1 | 8 | 7 | 2 | 5 |
| 5 | 7 | 3 | 9 | 2 | 6 | 1 | 4 | 8 |
| 3 | 6 | 2 | 8 | 9 | 5 | 4 | 1 | 7 |
| 1 | 5 | 7 | 6 | 4 | 3 | 8 | 9 | 2 |
| 9 | 8 | 4 | 2 | 7 | 1 | 5 | 6 | 3 |

## #25

| 2 | 1 | 5 | 9 | 3 | 4 | 8 | 7 | 6 |
| 3 | 7 | 8 | 2 | 6 | 5 | 1 | 4 | 9 |
| 9 | 4 | 6 | 7 | 8 | 1 | 5 | 3 | 2 |
| 6 | 8 | 4 | 1 | 7 | 9 | 3 | 2 | 5 |
| 7 | 9 | 3 | 8 | 5 | 2 | 6 | 1 | 4 |
| 1 | 5 | 2 | 6 | 4 | 3 | 9 | 8 | 7 |
| 8 | 3 | 7 | 4 | 9 | 6 | 2 | 5 | 1 |
| 4 | 6 | 1 | 5 | 2 | 8 | 7 | 9 | 3 |
| 5 | 2 | 9 | 3 | 1 | 7 | 4 | 6 | 8 |

## #26

| 8 | 7 | 6 | 3 | 4 | 2 | 1 | 9 | 5 |
| 5 | 2 | 1 | 9 | 7 | 8 | 6 | 3 | 4 |
| 9 | 3 | 4 | 6 | 5 | 1 | 7 | 8 | 2 |
| 1 | 8 | 9 | 7 | 3 | 5 | 2 | 4 | 6 |
| 4 | 5 | 3 | 2 | 1 | 6 | 8 | 7 | 9 |
| 7 | 6 | 2 | 8 | 9 | 4 | 5 | 1 | 3 |
| 2 | 9 | 5 | 4 | 8 | 7 | 3 | 6 | 1 |
| 6 | 4 | 8 | 1 | 2 | 3 | 9 | 5 | 7 |
| 3 | 1 | 7 | 5 | 6 | 9 | 4 | 2 | 8 |

# ANAGRAM

## #1

| | | | |
|---|---|---|---|
| LPEPA | APPLE | HICRA | CHAIR |
| ANECD | DANCE | LGIHT | LIGHT |
| LMEIS | SMILE | NCEDA | OCEAN |
| BCHAE | BEACH | CULOD | CLOUD |
| PAHYP | HAPPY | HNCLU | LUNCH |
| ESHOU | HOUSE | UMICS | MUSIC |
| EGRIT | TIGER | NLAPT | PLANT |
| AEWRT | WATER | BIRTBA | RABBIT |
| ELMNO | LEMON | CLCOK | CLOCK |
| RBADE | BREAD | OHSER | HORSE |
| AROCTR | CARROT | RSTSA | STARS |
| OBSKO | BOOKS | MYOEN | MONEY |
| YLLEJ | JELLY | ELISD | SLIDE |
| MEAPL | MAPLE | TWEES | SWEET |
| LTABE | TABLE | TNAIP | PAINT |
| RASSG | GRASS | GTIHN | NIGHT |
| URCTK | TRUCK | EUNEQ | QUEEN |
| RRIVE | RIVER | OUSEM | MOUSE |
| TUIEQ | QUIET | RAHET | EARTH |
| SILNA | SNAIL | ABSEN | BEANS |
| HCPAE | PEACH | ESDSR | DRESS |
| GAELN | ANGEL | INWSG | SWING |
| OHESS | SHOES | JIECU | JUICE |
| HLSEL | SHELL | SYNUN | SUNNY |
| GMNOA | MANGO | DCANY | CANDY |
| GSAERP | GRAPES | APPRE | PAPER |
| RAHET | HEART | ZIAPZ | PIZZA |
| YRTOS | STORY | HTWCA | WATCH |
| NKESA | SNAKE | DLCHI | CHILD |
| LRAIT | TRAIL | YEALF | LEAFY |

## #2

| | | | |
|---|---|---|---|
| ZBEREE | BREEZE | TUERBT | BUTTER |
| MCAAER | CAMERA | DCLAEN | CANDLE |
| EDEFFC | COFFEE | CIEOKO | COOKIE |
| ODCORT | DOCTOR | LRLDOA | DOLLAR |
| ERWFOL | FLOWER | IUARGT | GUITAR |
| MEARHM | HAMMER | CAKETJ | JACKET |
| NLUJEG | JUNGLE | TTRELE | LETTER |
| ORIMRR | MIRROR | EGRONA | ORANGE |
| EPLICN | PENCIL | OERTKC | ROCKET |
| LRESVI | SILVER | OSEKCT | SOCKET |
| KTECIT | TICKET | MELUBALR | UMBRELLA |
| WWIDNO | WINDOW | ANAANB | BANANA |
| BOLTET | BOTTLE | RYEHRC | CHERRY |
| ECRCLI | CIRCLE | EGDANR | DANGER |
| EDRNNI | DINNER | INEENG | ENGINE |
| YLMFAI | FAMILY | ERGAND | GARDEN |
| GREPSA | GRAPES | GOISLO | IGLOOS |
| ETICNS | INSECT | WJEEL | JEWEL |
| JWIGAS | JIGSAW | ALDRDE | LADDER |
| PPOATL | LAPTOP | ONELM | LEMON |

## #3

| | | | |
|---|---|---|---|
| ARLDIZ | LIZARD | PMLAE | MAPLE |
| UMIFNF | MUFFIN | ONNTAI | NATION |
| EEDLEN | NEEDLE | IOFECF | OFFICE |
| OVILE | OLIVE | PCAALE | PALACE |
| PTAORR | PARROT | BLPBEE | PEBBLE |
| EOPTKC | POCKET | BIBRAT | RABBIT |
| IARWOBN | RAINBOW | RLLREO | ROLLER |
| SNMOLA | SALMON | EAGSAUS | SAUSAGE |
| SWHAOD | SHADOW | SARHK | SHARK |
| IRSENG | SINGER | RCCSOE | SOCCER |
| RITPIS | SPIRIT | RASSIT | STAIRS |
| OMTTOA | TOMATO | RUTTLE | TURTLE |
| VEEVTL | VELVET | LESEVS | VESSEL |
| LAWETL | WALLET | SEWRHA | WASHER |
| TWOBAM | WOMBAT | IRTWER | WRITER |
| LLWYEO | YELLOW | IPEZPR | ZIPPER |
| OASRNC | ACORNS | ARTSTI | ARTIST |
| VBREEA | BEAVER | TACLES | CASTLE |
| CUSICR | CIRCUS | CISKEOO | COOKIES |
| ODANMID | DIAMOND | HMEULI | HELIUM |

## #4

| | | | |
|---|---|---|---|
| AYSBS | ABYSS | TUEAC | ACUTE |
| AEGLI | AGILE | AAJR | AJAR |
| ELPMA | AMPLE | GYARN | ANGRY |
| IRAD | ARID | ESANTC | ASCENT |
| ERAUG | AUGER | BLVEE | BEVEL |
| BANLD | BLAND | BLNUT | BLUNT |
| BIKRS | BRISK | DOBRO | BROOD |
| UNACJ | CAJUN | CAPRE | CAPER |
| HCOAS | CHAOS | CLTEF | CLEFT |
| EOVCL | CLOVE | GCNLU | CLUNG |
| XAOC | COAX | RISPC | CRISP |
| MBRCU | CRUMB | SCUTR | CRUST |
| IPCUD | CUPID | YNICC | CYNIC |
| DNDYA | DANDY | TUDNA | DAUNT |
| DCYOE | DECOY | URMDE | DEMUR |
| IRDVE | DIVER | TDFRA | DRAFT |
| DTFRI | DRIFT | OLLRD | DROLL |
| ENDOR | DRONE | ECITD | EDICT |
| OVEEK | EVOKE | LTEXA | EXALT |
| TNAFI | FAINT | KFLCI | FLICK |
| FUKEL | FLUKE | LYOFL | FOLLY |
| OFAYR | FORAY | UEFGD | FUDGE |
| NIFGU | FUNGI | IDDGY | GIDDY |
| TLGNI | GLINT | OOLMG | GLOOM |
| FRGUF | GRUFF | HEATS | HASTE |
| NIHGE | HINGE | ODHAR | HOARD |
| HNAYE | HYENA | CICLIE | ICICLE |
| LOGIO | IGLOO | BMIUE | IMBUE |
| AENIN | INANE | NTRIE | INERT |
| IUXFLN | INFLUX | UNAJT | JAUNT |

## SQUARE SUM #1

| | | | | |
|---|---|---|---|---|
| 3 | + | 9 | ÷ | 2 | → 6
| + | ■ | + | ■ | + |
| 6 | − | 1 | × | 8 | → 40
| × | ■ | + | ■ | |
| 5 | + | 4 | − | 7 | → 2

45    14    70

## SQUARE SUM #2

| | | | | |
|---|---|---|---|---|
| 4 | − | 3 | × | 5 | → 5
| + | ■ | + | ■ | + |
| 6 | − | 1 | − | 2 | → 3
| − | ■ | × | ■ | ÷ |
| 8 | + | 9 | × | 7 | → 119

2    36    1

## SQUARE SUM #3

| | | | | |
|---|---|---|---|---|
| 8 | + | 6 | × | 9 | → 126
| − | ■ | + | ■ | + |
| 7 | + | 2 | − | 4 | → 5
| + | ■ | × | ■ | + |
| 1 | + | 3 | × | 5 | → 20

2    24    18

## SQUARE SUM #4

| | | | | |
|---|---|---|---|---|
| 1 | + | 5 | + | 8 | → 14
| + | ■ | + | ■ | + |
| 4 | + | 6 | × | 2 | → 20
| − | ■ | × | ■ | − |
| 3 | + | 7 | + | 9 | → 19

2    77    1

## SQUARE SUM #5

| | | | | |
|---|---|---|---|---|
| 9 | + | 8 | × | 2 | → 34
| + | ■ | + | ■ | + |
| 5 | − | 1 | + | 3 | → 7
| + | ■ | × | ■ | × |
| 4 | + | 6 | × | 7 | → 70

18    54    35

## SQUARE SUM #6

| | | | | |
|---|---|---|---|---|
| 7 | − | 1 | × | 4 | → 24
| + | ■ | + | ■ | + |
| 8 | + | 5 | × | 3 | → 39
| × | ■ | + | ■ | × |
| 9 | − | 6 | − | 2 | → 1

135    12    14

## SQUARE SUM #7

| | | | | |
|---|---|---|---|---|
| 2 | + | 5 | × | 6 | 42 |
| - | ■ | + | ■ | + |
| 1 | + | 3 | × | 7 | 28 |
| × | ■ | ÷ | ■ | × |
| 8 | + | 4 | + | 9 | 21 |

8    12    117

## SQUARE SUM #8

| | | | | |
|---|---|---|---|---|
| 8 | + | 4 | × | 9 | 108 |
| + | ■ | + | ■ | - |
| 7 | + | 1 | - | 3 | 5 |
| ÷ | ■ | + | ■ | ÷ |
| 5 | + | 6 | + | 2 | 13 |

3    11    3

## SQUARE SUM #9

| | | | | |
|---|---|---|---|---|
| 8 | - | 7 | + | 3 | 4 |
| + | ■ | - | ■ | + |
| 9 | - | 2 | × | 5 | 35 |
| × | ■ | × | ■ | + |
| 4 | + | 1 | + | 6 | 11 |

68    5    2

## SQUARE SUM #10

| | | | | |
|---|---|---|---|---|
| 1 | + | 6 | × | 9 | 63 |
| + | ■ | + | ■ | + |
| 8 | - | 3 | × | 5 | 25 |
| - | ■ | × | ■ | ÷ |
| 4 | + | 2 | × | 7 | 42 |

5    18    2

## SQUARE SUM #11

| | | | | |
|---|---|---|---|---|
| 6 | + | 8 | - | 5 | 9 |
| + | ■ | + | ■ | + |
| 1 | + | 2 | × | 3 | 9 |
| × | ■ | - | ■ | + |
| 4 | + | 9 | × | 7 | 91 |

28    1    15

## SQUARE SUM #12

| | | | | |
|---|---|---|---|---|
| 9 | + | 5 | + | 3 | 17 |
| + | ■ | + | ■ | + |
| 6 | - | 4 | × | 8 | 16 |
| × | ■ | × | ■ | + |
| 1 | + | 7 | ÷ | 2 | 4 |

15    63    13

## WORD TRAIN #1

PORTRAIT, LANDSCAPE, CAMERA, LENS, ZOOM, EDITING, LIGHTING, FRAMING, FLASH, SHUTTER SPEED, FOCUS, TRIPOD

## WORD TRAIN #2

EASEL, BRUSH, CANVAS, OIL PAINT, WATERCOLOR, PLEIN AIR, SKETCH, PALETTE, PORTRAIT, LANDSCAPE, STILL LIFE

## WORD TRAIN #3

TROLLEY, CASHIER, DISCOUNT, DEALS, COUPONS, CREDIT CARD, CLEARANCE, PURCHASE, GIFT CARD, STORE, RETURNS

## WORD TRAIN #4

GOAL KEEPER, FIFA, STADIUM, SUBSTITUTE, REFEREE, MID-FIELD, HALF TIME, YELLOW CARD, CORNER, NET, DEFENDER

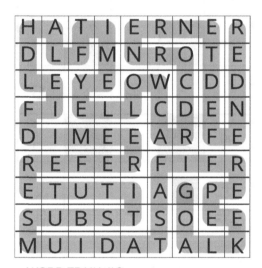

## WORD TRAIN #5

TURKEY, FEAST, PUMPKIN, HOLIDAY, NOVEMBER, GRATITUDE, FAMILY, PARADES, GATHER, BLESSINGS, HARVEST, FALL

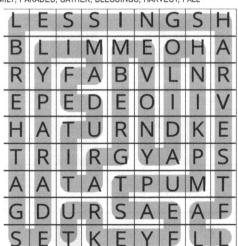

## WORD TRAIN #6

SAND, FLIPFLOP, SEASHELLS, TIDE, BIKINI, WAVES, SUNSCREEN, HAMMOCK, SEAGULLS, BOARDWALK, DUNES, TANNING

# LITTLE WORDS

JOURNEY:
ENJOY, JOUR, JURY, JOY, NERO, ONE, ONER, ORE, OUR, RYE, URN, YOU, YOUR, YEN, EURO, EON, OYER, RUE, YORE, YOURN, NO, NOR, OR, RUN

DELIGHT:
DELI, EIGHT, DIE, DIET, DIG, EDIT, GEL, GET, GILD, GILT, GLIDE, HE, HELD, HI, HIDE, HILT, HILTED, HIT, IDLE, LED, LEG, LEGIT, LET, LID, LIE, LIED, LIGHT, LIGHTED, LIT, LITHE, TIDE, TIE, TIED, TILDE, TILE, TILED

BLUEPRINT:
BE, BELT, BENT, BERLIN, BET, BIEN, BIT, BITE, BLIP, BLUE, BLUER, BLUNT, BLUNTER, BLUR, BLURT, BRINE, BRUT, BRUTE, BUILT, BUN, BUNTER, BURT, BURN, BURNT, BURP, BUT, BUTLER, ERUPT, INEPT, INERT, INLET, INPUT, INTEL, INTER, LENT, IT, LEPT, LEPTIN, LIE, LIER, LIEU, LINER, LINEUP, LIP, PUB, PUN, PUNT, PURE, PURINE, REBUILT, REIN, RENT, RIB, RIP, RIPE, RIPEN, RITE, RUB, RUBLE, RUE, RUIN, RULE, RUN, RUT, TIRE, TRIBE, TRIBUNE, TRIP, TRIPLE, TRUE, TUB, TUBER, TULIP, TUNE, TUNER, TURBINE, TURN, TURNIP, UNITE, UNIT, UNLIT, UNRIP, UNRIPE, UNTIE, UNTIL, UP, URINE, URN

DAUGHTER:
AD, AGE, AGED, ARE, ARGH, ARGUE, ART, AUGER, DART, DATE, DATER, DEAR, DEARTH, DEATH, DRAG, DRAUGHT, DRUG, DUE, DUET, DUG, DUH, EAR, EARTH, EAT, ERA, ETA, GATE, GATED, GATHER, GEAR, GET, GRAD, GRADE, GRATE, GRATED, GREAT, GRUE, GUARD, HAD, HARD, HARE, HART, HAT, HATE, HATED, HATER, HATRED, HE, HEAD, HEAR, HEARD, HEART, HEAT, HER, HERD, HUE, HUG, HUGE, HUGER, HURT, HUT, RAD, RAG, RAGE, RAGED, RAT, RATE, RATED, READ, RED, REDHAT, RETAG, RUDE, RUE, RUED, RUG, RUT, TOE, TAG, TAR, TARE, TARED, TEA, TEAR, THREAD, THE, THUD, THUG, TRADE, TREAD, TRUE, TURD, UGH, URATE, UREAT, URGE, URGED

BLUNDER:
BE, BED, BEN, BEND, BLED, BLEND, BLUE, BLUED, BLUR, BRED, BUD, BUN, BUNDLE, BUNDLER, BUR, BURDEN, BURN, BURNED, DEBLUR, DEN, DRUB, DUB, DUE, DUEL, DUNE, END, LED, LEND, LEUD, LUBE, LUBED, LURE, LURED, NERD, NUDE, NURD, RED, RUB, RUBE, RUDE, RUE, RUED, RULE, RULED, RUN, UNBRED, UNDER, UNLED, URN

ABSOLVE:
ABLE, ABOVE, ABS, ALOE, ALSO, BAE, BALE, BALES, BASE, EBOLA, LAB, LABS, LAVE, LOAVES, LOB, LOBE, LOBES, LOSE, LOVE, LOVES, OVAL, OVALS, SALE, SALVE, SEA, SEAL, SLAB, SLAVE, SLOB, SOB, VASE

SECURITY:
CITE, CITES, CITERS, CITRUS, CITRUSY, CITY, CREST, CRIES, CRUISE, CRUISY, CRUST, CRUSTY, CRY, CUE, CUES, CURE, CURES, CURET, CURETS, CURSE, CURTSY, CUT, CUTE, CUTER, CUTES, CUTESY, CUTIE, CUTIES, CUTS, CYST, ERST, ICE, ICES, ICY, IRE, IRES, IS, IT, ITER, ITS, RECTUS, RECUT, REST, RICE, RISE, RITE, RITES, RUE, RUES, RUSE, RUST, RUSTIC

HOSPITAL:
TOPSAIL, PATHOS, POLISH, POTASH, LATISH, LITHOS, PATIOS, PILOTS, PISTOL, POSTAL, PLAITS, SPOILT, PATHS, PITHS, HAILS, HALOS, HALTS, HILTS, HOIST, LATHI, LITHO, LOATH, OATHS, SLOTH, THALI, HIPS, HOPS, PATH, PITH, SHIP, POSH, SHOP, HAIL, HALO, HALT, HATS, HILT, OATH, SHIT, SHAT, SHOT, HIP, HOP, HAS, HAT, HIS, HIT, HOT, APT, LIP, LAP, PAT, PAL, PIT, POT, HI, TO

TRUNCATE:
UNCRATE, UNTRACE, TAUNTER, ACUTER, CENTRA, CURATE, CUTTER, NECTAR, TRANCE, UNCART, ATTUNE, NATURE, NUTTER, ACUTE, CARET, CARTE, CATER, CRANE, CRATE, CUTER, ENACT, TRACE, TRUCE, TAUNT, TREAT, TUNER, UTTER, ACER, ACNE, ACRE, CANE, CANT, CARE, CART, CENT, CUNT, CURE, RACE, TACT, AUNT, NEAR, NEAT, RANT, RATE, RENT, RUNT, TARN, ACE, ACT, ARC, CAN, CAR, CAT, CUE, CUT, ANT, ARE, ART, ATE, EAR, EAT, ERA, RAN, RAT, RUN, RT, TEA, TEN

PLUMBERS:
REPLUMBS, BUMPERS, PLUMBER, REPLUMB, LUMBERS, LUMPERS, RUMBLES, SLUMBER, BUMPER, BLUMES, LUMBER, RUMBLE, SUPERB, PULSER, PLUMB, BLUME, BURPS, LUMPS, BUMPS, PERMS, PLUMS, SLUMP, SPERM, LEMUR, LUBES, MULES, PULSE, PURSE, PURES, REBUS, BUMP, BURP, PLUM, BLUE, BLUR, MUSE, PLUS, PURE, REPS, BUM, PUB, ELM, EMU, RUM, SUM, BUS, SUE, SUM, RUE, BE, ME, US

BACKGROUNDS:
BACKGROUND, RUNBACKS, SOUNDBAR, UNDOCKS, UNBARKS, UNCORKS, ABSCOND, CARBONS, CANDOUR, COUGARS, DRAGONS, GROUNDS, UNDOCK, UNCORK, BACONS, CARBON, COBRAS, ABSURD, BACKS, BUCKS, DOCKS, BANKS, BURKA, CONKS, CORKS, CRANK, CROAK, RACKS, RUCKS, ROCKS, SNUCK, DANKS, DORKS, BACK, BUCK, DOCK, DUCK, GACK, BANK, BARK, BASK, CORK, KNOB, RACK, ROCK, SACK, SOCK, SUCK, DARK, DORK, ACK, ASK, CAB, OAK, BAD, BAG, BUD, BUG, COD, DUB, ABS, ARC, BAN, BAR, NO, ON, AS, US

THIS IS A LIST OF FEW COMMON WORDS, NOT THE COMPLETE
POSSIBLE LIST !!

# CITY LIMITS

Paris - France
Tokyo - Japan
New York City - United States
London - United Kingdom
Beijing - China
Moscow - Russia
Sydney - Australia
Rome - Italy
Cairo - Egypt
Rio de Janeiro - Brazil
Istanbul - Turkey
Mumbai - India
Berlin - Germany
Dubai - United Arab Emirates
Buenos Aires - Argentina
Seoul - South Korea
Toronto - Canada
Mexico City - Mexico
Johannesburg - South Africa
Bangkok - Thailand
Singapore - Singapore
Madrid - Spain
Amsterdam - Netherlands
Jakarta - Indonesia
Nairobi - Kenya
New Delhi - India
Los Angeles - United States
Athens - Greece
Stockholm - Sweden
Vienna - Austria

Jersey City, New Jersey
Albany, New York
Chicago, Illinois
Houston, Texas
Phoenix, Arizona
Philadelphia, Pennsylvania
San Antonio, Texas
San Diego, California
New Haven, Connecticut
Providence, Rhode Island
Atlanta, Georgia
Jacksonville, Florida
San Francisco, California
Indianapolis, Indiana
Columbus, Ohio
Fort Worth, Texas
Charlotte, North Carolina
Seattle, Washington
Denver, Colorado
Washington, D.C.
Boston, Massachusetts
El Paso, Texas
Nashville, Tennessee
Detroit, Michigan
Portland, Oregon
Memphis, Tennessee
Oklahoma City, Oklahoma
Las Vegas, Nevada
Baltimore, Maryland
Louisville, Kentucky

# TRIVIA LADDER

FIRST VOWEL - A
CHEMICAL SYMBOL FOR GOLD - AU
OPPOSITE OF COLD - HOT
ABBREVIATION FOR PREOFESSOR - PROF
THE BLUE PLANET - EARTH
WHEN MIXED WITH BLUE MAKES GREEN - YELLOW
LARGEST OCEAN ON EARTH - PACIFIC
CAPITAL CITY OF AUSTRALIA - CANBERRA
FIVE-POINTED STAR - PENTAGRAM
WORDS THAT READ THE SAME WHEN READ BACKWARD - PALINDROME

ANS: BILL CLINTON

FIRST CONSONANT - B
REFERS TOT HE YEARS AFTER BIRTH OF JESUS - AD
THE STAR AROUND WHICH THE EARTH ORBITS - SUN
PLANET KNOWN AS THE "RED PLANET" - MARS
A SWEET, VISCOUS FOOD SUBSTANCE MADE BY BEES - HONEY
ONE OF THE WORLD'S LARGEST DESERT - SAHARA
SIX - SIDED POLYGON - HEXAGON
FIVE - SIDED POLYGON - PENTAGON
DECREASE IN PRICE IN ECONOMY - DEFLATION
GROUP OF DRUGS USED TO REDUCE SENSATION DURING SURGERY - ANESTHESIA

ANS: USAIN BOLT

LAST ALPHABET - Z
ABBREVIATION OF CALIFORNIA - CA
DIAGRAMMATIC REPRESENTATION OF A GEOGRAPHY - MAP
LARGEST CONTINENT - ASIA
MUSICAL INSTRUMENT PLAYED USING A KEYBOARD - PIANO
RINGED PLANET - SATURN
BIRD WITH BEAUTIFUL TAIL FEATHERS - PEACOCK
THE GALAXY WE LIVE IN - MILKY WAY
RETURNS TO THE THROWER WHEN THROWN - BOOMERANG
WHAT AMAZON IS - RAIN FOREST

ANS: TOM CRUISE

FIRST PERSON SINGULAR PRONOUN - I
ABBREVIATION FOR THE STATE OF TEXAS - TX
THIS IS MIGHTIER THAN THE SWORD - PEN
BIRD KNOWN FOR ITS DISTINCTIVE 'CAW-CAW' SOUN - CROW
THE LARGEST MAMMAL IN THE WORLD, WHICH LIVES IN THE OCEAN - WHALE
BIRD KNOWN FOR ITS ABILITY TO MIMIC HUMAN SPEECH - PARROT
WORLD'S HIGHEST MOUNTAIN - EVEREST
GRASSY PLAIN WITH FEW TREES - SAVANNAH
MIB ACTOR - WILL SMITH
A PERSON WHO PRACTICES ASTROLOGY - ASTROLOGER

ANS: TRAMPOLINES

Thank you so much!!

Thank you for buying "The Smart Teenager" and attempting to solve the puzzles..
I hope the puzzles are engaging.

If you find this book of puzzles interesting, please consider leaving an honest review for the book on Amazon. As a budding independent publisher, your one review would mean the world to me. It does wonders to the book and I would also love to hear your experience.

To leave your feedback:
1. Open your Camera app
2. Point your mobile device at the QR Code
3. The review page will appear in your web browser

Scan me

Or
Visit - https://bit.ly/432MBw7

- ELAN H

Made in United States
Cleveland, OH
09 December 2024

11573894R00057